MW00877071

UNDEFEATED UNTIED UNSCORED UPON

The story of Pennsylvania's 1957 Cass Township Football Team

JIM DROSKINIS

THANK YOU

to the many folks who made this book possible. If details are correct, it is thanks to *your* conscientious efforts.

If facts are wrong - it is *my* fault!

Printed by CreateSpace, An Amazon.com Company

Available from Amazon.com and other online stores

Available on Kindle and other devices

Copyright © 2017 Jim Droskinis

All rights reserved.

ISBN-13: 978-1974125142

ISBN-10: 1974125149

DEDICATION

Coach Pat Droskinis
(1915-1999)

I am very pleased this story is finally being told. My dad would have loved to edit this book and add color, commentary and details. The old coach would have made it *much* better! He'd have added many stories, and filled in details lost to sports history. He lived to play sports, teach, coach, officiate and to tell tales, especially sports stories. He certainly would have made this compilation much more interesting. And more fun to read. Then it would have been a best-seller for sure! (Kidding.)

Pat had that unique Pennsylvania coal country knack for running into a group of strangers - and leaving a bunch of friends. He was an exceptional man. A really good story teller. (Most of the stories were even true.)

I miss him every day!

Table of Contents

1957 Cass Football Team

L to R, Frantz, Hydock, Gauntlett, Gressik, Coach Droskinis, Ryan, Heffron, Kachmar, Butsko; 2nd row, Machita, Brennan, Zurat, Yuschock, Phillips, Krasnitsky, Ney, Milyo, Antonelli; 3rd row, Witcofsky, Hinners, Wenner, Zurat, Gretsky, Sinko, Mitchell, Callaghan, Stevens; 4th row, Hardock, Oakill, Kurtak, Mitchell, Onusko, Kessler, Heffron, Jefferson, Slane; 5th row, managers, Klutonovich, Mabry

FORWARD

Writing a book is a team sport. For many years I sat at my desk in Georgia, or overseas in Iraq and Afghanistan, writing whenever I could, but I felt like a ship's captain in charge of a trip to nowhere. I originally intended to do way too much. That is until now!

As promised, with readers help and kind advice, I am now telling this story by doing only what I know how to do, within the limitations of how I can do it. Let me explain what this book is not. It is not fiction, not a love story, and does not have fake characters. It is just a *true* Pennsylvania coal region sports story. I explain the game-by-game progress in a unique fun way.

I hope this book evokes some strong memories both for the unselfish players and for the families of the Cass players who have already passed. And I have confidence that sports fans around the country will surely appreciate the amazing accomplishments and teamwork of this underfunded, *Cinderella* football team. No matter where you are, I hope you can relate some of the sports action to your local teams. And to the character of coaches you have known in your cities and towns.

This story is told mostly from the Cass team's point of view, but I mean no insult to anyone from the towns whose proud teams Cass beat that year, 1957. In fact, I respect them. After all, I *am* a 1971 graduate from one of those small towns that Cass crushed - Minersville Area High School.

Remember, this is only the first edition, so the book may be about a perfect season, but this is not a perfect book. There will be a second edition with updates, corrections, new pictures, and more information about the players' lives.

Finally, a challenge: this book provides a perfect foundation for someone to write a screenplay. I see a "based on" fictionalized version of **UNDEFEATED UNTIED UNSCORED UPON** as a hit movie!

Chapter 1

Coach Pat Dreams

The year was 1999. Pennsylvania Sports Hall of Fame coach Pat Droskinis was 83 years old and lay in his bed drifting in and out of consciousness. The old coach knew he was dying of cancer, but wasn't ready to call it quits. Not yet! He had whipped prostate cancer into remission twelve years prior, but the disease returned with a vengeance. Lucid moments at this stage were rare, and he knew his days were numbered. Still, he kept the faith.

Suddenly, some familiar voices and noises startled him. He opened his eyes and saw a few of his favorite football players. Gathered at his bedside were members of the legendary Cass Township championship football team that he coached back in the late 1950s.

The men started swapping memories of football games about their longtime friend, coach, and mentor. Eventually, Pat was awake enough to speak and join in too, adding some jokes and zingers. But after an hour or so, the pain medication kicked in. The coach closed his eyes and drifted back to sleep.

With his boys (now older men) by his hospice bedside, Coach Pat held court with his team one last time from his dream state. Although they had watched the old black and white 16 mm championship game film together many times at team reunions and banquets, this last time was special. The pain meds made it real for Pat. Call it magic, call it chemistry. The imaginary projector clicked ON.

All of a sudden, Coach Pat was a younger man of 42 years and his players were young men between ages 15 and 18 again. They had all traveled back in time to December 7th, 1957, the 16th anniversary of Pearl Harbor Day. It was a cold, dreary, rainy, Saturday afternoon. It had snowed earlier that week and the ground was frozen. That is, until the day before, when it had warmed up and started to rain. By game day, the frozen tundra of a football field had turned into a giant sea of mud. The ankle-deep, muddy field was speckled with white snow.

Two great high school football teams in the coal regions of Pennsylvania were about to face off at Pottsville's Veterans Memorial Stadium. It was a special play-off game for the championship of the Southern Division of the Eastern Conference. Cass Township, undefeated, with a 9-0 record, the tiny coal patch school with only enough players to do half-line scrimmages, was about to have a championship match-up with Shamokin, a much larger regional school with 10 wins and 2 losses.

Fewer than two-thousand fans braved the bad weather to witness this epic showdown. Thousands of others stayed in the warmth of their homes and listened to the live radio broadcast. But if you listened to talk of the folks from Schuylkill County years later, there surely must have been 10,000 people or more at the game. "I was there that day," said most all of the old timers. In fact, over the years, many folks from the Minersville or Cass Township area either claimed to play on that legendary team, or had a cousin that did. That's okay; a little mythology might be in order. This game was one of the most amazing games in Pennsylvania sports history.

And what a match-up! Indeed, it was battle to the end. The half-time score was 0-0. Both teams' uniforms were so muddy, you could hardly tell one team from another. Shamokin came back out from the locker room for the third quarter with nice clean white jerseys. But the coal miners' sons from Cass Township didn't have any other maroon jerseys. They stood under the hot showers at halftime in full uniforms to wash off most of the mud. So they emerged into the cold with wet uniforms. As it turned out, they didn't need any clean or fancy equipment. They had all that they needed to win - sheer determination.

The third quarter ended and the game was still scoreless. In the cold rain and mud, any consistent offensive assault by either team was almost impossible. But what a ball game! Some Cass fans sensed that sports history was in the making. Could something miraculous happen? Forty-seven minutes, forty-five seconds had now ticked off the clock and the score was still tied at 0-0. Never give up!

The cold rain continued and it seemed hopeless that either team could score on this slippery battlefield. Now with only 15 seconds on the clock, it was 4th down and Shamokin was trapped back near their five yard line.

What to do? The Cass Condors could play it safe, just let the Shamokin Greyhounds punt and focus on a clean catch of the ball in the wet conditions. Then they would have a few seconds left to attempt a final play to score. If they failed, it would still be a tie. There would still be plenty of glory in that feat.

Remember, going into the championship game, the Cass Condors were not only "undefeated," but also "untied," as well as "unscored upon!" The sports writers of the local paper (*The Pottsville Republican)* did not even use the term "unscored upon" until late in the season. They just said Cass held all their opponents *scoreless.*

Back to the final seconds. It was 4th down on a messy, muddy, wet, and bone-chilling football game. The Shamokin Greyhounds were in a quandary, as they were trapped on their own five yard line. They lined up in punt formation, and time stopped. Tick tock! Then the ball was snapped and the seconds ticked away. The Cass defensive line rushed with a fury, concentration, determination and intensity known only to the most fervent of competitors.

No one was exactly sure what was going to happen. But Pat's team knew that somehow, someway, they had to block that punt. Shamokin's Jerry Haupt athletically handled the soggy, low-snapped football from his center. THUD! He punted it as hard as he could - but Russ Frantz, Tony Phillips, Steve Kachmar, Gus Gressik, Harry Butsko, Joe Hydock, Charlie Zurat and the Cass defensive unit "rushed like hell," as Pat would say!

Little did Jerry know that a Cass youngster, only in his junior year, Joe Hydock, a big kid, about 205 pounds, would reach as high as humanly possible and cleanly block the football with part of his left hand, mere inches from the punter's extended right foot.

Bouncing footballs do strange things. This one shot right back toward Shamokin's end zone, and Russ Frantz, Cass team co-captain, tried desperately to grab the muddy ball before it rolled out of the end zone, for a touchdown. However, it rolled off his cold and wet fingertips and out of the end zone near a bank of piled up muddy snow. That was okay as a safety still counts for 2 points. The Cass players looked around and were stunned. No one was exactly sure what happened or knew at the time who blocked the punt. They did not really care, as the scoreboard now read Cass 2, Shamokin 0 (Actually, *"PHS 2"* - *"VIS"* 0). Everyone looked around. There were no penalties from the game officials.

Russ Frantz yelled out, "Joey did it," meaning Joe Hydock blocked the punt. The fans, now all standing in the 40 degree rain, did not feel cold or wet - just shock and disbelief.

Essentially the game was over. However, football rules state that "after a safety is scored, the ball is kicked off to the team that scored the safety from the 20-yd line." So Shamokin, down by two points, had to kick off to Cass with only a few seconds left.

The Greyhound kickoff in the mud did not go very far, but it was indeed still a live ball and Cass had to handle it. Shamokin must have had desperate hopes of grabbing it and taking it all the way for a touchdown. Beakley Ryan fell on the football and just lay there as the game ended. The fans, all standing in the icy rain, now did not feel cold or wet - just astonishment and disbelief. The players hugged, jumped up and down, and shook hands while drifting toward the hot showers. Some smiled and remembered that a prearranged banquet at a warm, dry place in nearby Minersville called "Deer Park" awaited both the winning and losing teams that evening.

Naturally, the Cass faithful were ecstatic, elated, proud, and happy beyond belief and knew in an instant that they had done the impossible. Of course, Shamokin Coach Lou Sorrentino, the players, coaches, and their fans were stunned, shocked, and dejected, as their team had just played their hearts out, yet lost. But what no one could know at that moment in time is that Cass had just become a legend in Pennsylvania sports history.

That experience affected the rest of the Cass players' lives. In the decades that followed, the Cass team and its coach formed a sort of mystic bond, and most remained friends for life and went on to hold emotional team reunions.

The championship game itself certainly was one of destiny, and one for the ages. By shear guts, great teamwork, and faith in each other and support from their community, Cass completed the season with a perfect record. They scored a total of 223 points to zero by all opponents. They were "UNDEFEATED UNTIED and UNSCORED UPON."

Unbelievable? It really did happen! This book is the game-by-game story of how a football coach known as Coach Peter "Pat" Droskinis and a determined team of poor, teen-aged boys became local, reluctant sports "heroes," and teammates for life.

Chapter 2

The Setting: The 1950s

At the time of this historic season in the fall of 1957, America only had 48 states. Alaska was not admitted to the union until January 3, 1959. Hawaii became our 50th state on August 21, 1959

The 1950s were magical years: supposedly the good old days. The President for eight years was former WWII famous General Dwight D. "Ike" Eisenhower. His Vice President was none other than Mr. Dick Nixon - yes, the same Nixon who went on to become President Nixon in 1968. President Eisenhower's connection to football is that he played running back and linebacker for Army's West Point varsity in 1912. During the Cass football season, Ike suffered a stroke in November, 1957.

Earlier in 1957, the late, great Humphrey Bogart died. And just what kind of movies was America watching back then? How about Jimmy Stewart in *The Spirit of St Louis,* Henry Fonda in *12 Angry Men, An Affair to Remember* with Cary Grant, *A Farewell to Arms* with Rock Hudson, *The Curse of Frankenstein,* with Peter Cushing, and a famous "B" movie classic - *I Was a Teenage Werewolf,* starring Michael Landon. Other popular movies were *Gunfight at the O.K. Corral,* starring Kirk Douglas and Burt Lancaster, *Jailhouse Rock,* with, of course, Elvis Presley (premiered the exact same day Cass beat Blythe Township 35-0), *Bridge on the River Kwai* with William Holden and Alec Guinness. And most of us oldsters cried when we saw the movie *Old Yeller* starring Fess Parker.

What about television? There were some real classics and some real corny shows on the (black and white) small tube! Here are a few (some still on cable re-runs). *I Love Lucy, The Ed Sullivan Show, General Electric Theatre, The $64,000 Question, The Millionaire, The Red Skelton Show, Father Knows Best, The Lone Ranger, Bonanza,* and *Gunsmoke* (#1 rated show for the next three years). The iconic, idealistic, stereotypical 1950s show -

Leave It to Beaver, debuted in October of 1957. Other shows included *Zorro, The Dick Van Dyke Show, Captain Kangaroo, Candid Camera, Bozo the Clown*, and the late Dick Clark's classic - *American Bandstand*. Long before Johnny Carson and Jay Leno were household names, Jack Paar became the first permanent host of NBC's *The Tonight Show* on July 29, 1957.

As for the tiny patch in Pennsylvania known as Cass Township, life was simple and peaceful. Fewer than 2,000 folks lived in the township, and most eked out a tough living either in the coal mines or the textile factories. Some of the dads had served either in the Korean War, WWII, or both. Few owned the small black and white televisions from those days, but most had at least one radio. Nonetheless, for most, life was good, and the country had been at peace ever since the end of the Korean War in 1953.

Elvis was king of a new form of teenage madness called Rock and Roll. In the (AM, as there was no FM) radios in cars and homes you heard the likes of "*Whole Lotta Shakin' Going On*" by Jerry Lee Lewis, "*Jailhouse Rock*" by Elvis Presley, "*Peggy Sue*," by Buddy Holly, and "*Wake Up Little Susie*," by the Everly Brothers.

In many states, high school football was also king. In all fairness, baseball was still America's favorite pastime and the nation's sports fans had just focused on a stunning upset in the World Series. Maybe as if it were a prophecy for little Cass, MLB baseball's underdog Cinderella team, the Milwaukee Braves, defeated the mighty New York Yankees. They won the 1957 World Series in seven games. (Exactly a year prior to Cass High School's Perfect Season, Don Larsen threw the "perfect game" for the Yankees in the 1956 World Series (the famous Yogi Berra was his catcher).

And the Milwaukee Braves won, holding the Yankees to a total of *zero runs* in this mystical game seven. Hmmm - UNSCORED upon? The Braves had just won their first pennant since moving from Boston in 1953. They were led by hall of famers Warren Spahn, Hank Aaron, and Ed Mathews as well as Lew Burdette, Joe

Adcock and Del Crandall. The nation was enthralled listening to the World Series as game seven was played on Oct 10th, 1957. That very day, the mighty Cass football team would go on to win their 5th victory of the season, defeating Ashland, PA, 19-0. At that point in the season, opponents scored a total of zero points; Cass had scored 152!

Back to baseball: Ironically, do you know who lost game seven? Don Larsen, the winner of *the perfect game* just a year earlier! The 1957 World Series featured legends we have all come to know, including Yankee greats Mickey Mantle, Yogi Berra, Tony Kubek, Elston Howard, Whitey Ford, and Bobby Richardson.

Life was good. As for Pennsylvania names, Cass featured teenaged football players with names like Frantz, Gressik, Butsko, Heffron, Gauntlett, Zurat, Antonelli, Hydock, Machita, Brennan, Kachmar, Phillips, Pecovich, Krasnisky and Wannisky, to name a few. With those last names, you can tell what an ethnic melting pot Cass Township was! Irish, Polish, and Lithuanian to name a few. The names lend themselves to some cool nicknames that will be revealed later. Most everyone had a nickname back then.

One of the most intense competitive races ever was happening in the worldwide stage - not in sports, but in science - the race to space. On October 3rd, 1957 the former Soviet Union (now Russia) launched Sputnik into outer space, beating the United States and causing a kind of international disappointment. However, that very day on October 3rd, Cass beat Schuylkill Haven by the blowout score of 40-0. Local sports fans were really starting to get excited about their small town team's fourth shutout of the season, not just outer space. And remember, very few Americans had TVs in those days, but most listened on those scratchy old AM radios.

Car styles reflected the USA's fascination with rocket ships. One of the classic cars of all time, the 1957 Chevy, had two chrome "rocket ships" on the hood of the car. And how about all those big tail fins like a rocket ship that popped up on Cadillacs (see picture) and other automobiles: Chevrolets, Fords, Lincolns, and Plymouths to name a few.

As for pro football, Bart Starr was the legendary quarterback for the Green Bay Packers, and Sonny Jurgensen was the Philadelphia Eagles signal caller. The renowned Johnny Unitas had been playing for the Baltimore Colts since 1955. The 1957 season was the 38th regular season of the National Football League. The NFL season ended on Dec 29th, 1957 when the Detroit Lions crushed the Cleveland Browns in the NFL *Championship Game*, 59-14 (It was not called the Super Bowl yet). Yes, you know the name of the most famous player in that game: Syracuse University's former college star - Jim Brown.

Chapter 3

Cass Township

Cass Township is a very small ethnic town located in Schuylkill County, Pennsylvania along Interstate 81. Cass consists of only 14 square miles. It was formed in 1848 from part of Branch Township. Cass Township is named after Lewis Cass, a general in the War of 1812, governor of Michigan, Michigan U.S. senator, one time presidential candidate, and Secretary of State.

Cass achieved some historic footnotes during the Civil War. Here is a direct quote from the book, *The Valley We Loved so Well:* "Cass Township gained notoriety during the Civil War when the people protested the unfairness of the Conscription Act, which allowed the wealthy to buy their way out of the draft, thus making it a poor man's war. Trains were stopped in the township and conscripts were forced to get off. President Lincoln averted a disaster by not allowing the federal troops which had been sent to Pottsville from Harrisburg to enter the township, thus downplaying the seriousness of the protests and averting national negative publicity to center on the township."

Interesting? Following is some more history about Cass Township and the Civil War from the book, *Coal Mining, Draft*

Rioting & the Molly Maguires: From Laois to Schuylkill with the Delaney Family:

"The 1860 Census finds the (Delaney) family in the largely Irish Cass Township, Schuylkill County; Thomas and his eldest boys are all recorded as miners. One of the younger boys, Thomas Jr. (recorded as 15 in 1860) was just setting out on his mining career. Sometime that year he started work in the nearby Forestville mine. He joined some 1,590 miners who called Cass Township home in 1860, in a location that has been described as 'the most turbulent area in the anthracite region throughout the 1860s.' It would become a notorious location during the Civil War. Part of the reason for this was the fact that the miners were not afraid to organize themselves in order to achieve what they viewed as their working entitlements. This was nothing new; it was likely a propensity for organizing themselves that Samuel Lewis was alluding to when he noted in 1837 that the Rathaspick miners were 'particularly observant of every kind of holiday.'

"By 1862 the miners in Cass Township were fed up, and many went on strike in search of higher wages. The Militia were called in to restart the mine pumps, but were forced to withdraw when they were attacked by rioters. Eventually over 200 troops had to be summoned to quell the situation. Not long afterwards, the Militia Act of 17th July, 1862 authorized the implementation of state drafts to supply the Union with men. Again, Cass Township responded. Up to 1,000 miners marched to a nearby town, where they stopped a train load of draftees heading towards Harrisburg - troops were again needed to quieten the area. The miners were just as angry with their employers as they were with the draft. In December 1862, up to 200 armed men from Cass Township attacked the Phoenix Colliery, beating up a number of men connected with the mine's operations.

"The following March, when enrolling officers arrived in Schuylkill to record the names of men in the area for the Enrollment Act draft, they were driven off. One of the officers recalled how 'it was uncomfortably warm, as the Irish had congregated, and, as we found, were determined to resist, and did by giving us four shots from a revolver (luckily none hitting us).' Disturbances continued in the region throughout much of the war, and although they were by no means restricted to the Irish community, the Irish were frequently singled out as those culpable. Often exaggerated and almost hysterical reports were being sent to Washington. In July 1863 Brigadier - General Whipple reported that 'The miners of Cass Township, near Pottsville, have organized to resist the draft, the number of 2,500 or 3,000 armed men.' He also claimed they were drilling every evening, had artillery, and were commanded by returned soldiers.

"Eventually, the Provost Marshal sent officials backed with troops to seize the payrolls of mine operators, so their employees' names could be added to the draft. The events in the 1860s saw the continued rise in Schuylkill County of a secret organization known as the Molly Maguires, who would dramatically leap to prominence in the 1870s."

In 1957, Cass was a small town where just about everyone was poor, especially by today's standards. They just did *not know* they were poor because they came from hard working families who taught them values. They developed character and ethics that would last a lifetime.

Back then, many men still worked in the coal mines and a lot of women toiled in a local factory called *Jackson's Sportswear*

located near the high school. At the 50th Cass Reunion, Cass star player (NFL player) Harry Butsko said, "We were all so poor, even the poor kids called us *poor*." These were boys of good stock: As you can tell from the names mentioned above, their heritage was mixed: a lot of Irish, a few Italians, Polish, Ukrainians, Lithuanians, Germans, and Pennsylvania Dutch lived in the coal regions.

Cass Township High School was built in 1916 and continued for a half century. Due to declining enrollment, the school had to merge with Minersville High School in 1966. That last senior class only had 25 seniors. The *four year* academy course was started in 1919 and this placed the Cass High School on a higher academic level. In 1920 Cass Township High School was recognized as a first class high school. Students came from local patches: Greenbury, Coal Castle, Pine Knot, Cherry Valley, Hecksherville, Mackeysburg, Glen Carbon, Glen Dower, Thomaston, Mt. Pleasant, Buck Run, Jonestown, Black Heath, Forestville, and Primrose. If you are from the coal regions, you can relate to these small neighborhoods. If you are from other parts of the country, it may seem strange how these tiny communities retained their own identity and character.

Cass Township School did not have a football team until 1927.

The very first game was a victory over local school, Pine Grove. The stands and the lights were installed in 1948. Cass played against Minersville as their opening game under those lights and beat them 19-0. As to the giant light poles, they were eventually sold to St Clair in 1969 and generated a scholarship fund that distributed $57,000 to Minersville and Nativity High School graduating seniors for decades.

There were only 55 seniors in the class of 1958 (football year 1957). This number diminished steadily until 1966 when Cass High School shut its doors forever. The district merged with former sports rival Minersville. Cass Township High School fielded its last football team in 1964 with only 21 seniors in the class. They only played five games and finished 1-4. (The only team they beat was Marion Catholic by 20-7.)

A bunch of the kids from Cass hung out at a place called "Sophia's," owned by the sister of unofficial unpaid, assistant coach/trainer, Johnny Pytko. It was mostly harmless fun - they smoked a few cigarettes outside, drank sodas and talked about school, girls, mischief, and fun stuff teen age boys of all generations talk about. They took turns pumping nickels into the juke box listening to rock and roll records or 45 RPMs. It is even rumored that a few Yuenglings were consumed outside. Coincidentally, there just happened to be a bar down the street called "Popes!"

Cass Township had its own drive - in movie theatre back in the 1950s called Live Oaks Drive In. Sometimes the guys either paid a quarter by the carload or they sneaked in and sat along the coal banks, watched the giant screen, and listened to the speaker boxes on poles carved in the coal dirt, positioned near each car space. There was free swimming "at your own risk" available at a local clear water-filled old strip mine called Blue Dam, in nearby Mt. Pleasant.

Cass Township was a devout community. Most folks attended church on Sundays, and no one protested or was offended, when

Coach Pat led the team in prayer before each game - on the field in full view. He started, "Our Father who art in Heaven, hallowed be thy name," and the players all joined in. The Lord's Prayer was a part of each and every ballgame Cass played.

"If I should win, let it be by the code
With my Faith and my Honor held high.
If I should lose, let me stand by the road
And cheer as the winners go by."
(From the Cass Class of 1951)

23

Chapter 4

Secret Weapons

In 1957, Cass employed a *single wing* offense, a bit similar to today's shotgun formation, where the center snaps the ball to a back about five yards behind him - no quarterback's hands touching the center. In the single wing formation, the center snapped the ball between his legs, to any of *three* different backs, who ran, passed or handed off.

More on the single wing offense later, but without a great ball-snapper or center, there was no hope of playing this style of football. No chance of a perfect season. The first secret weapon was Cass center, an unsung hero named Dave Gauntlett. Dave was all of 145 pounds soaking wet, 5 feet 10 inches tall, and had to not only make snaps on target, but also had to block one or two defenders. For a lineman, he was undersized, even by 1950s standards, but played with amazing concentration and pride in his part of the football machine called the Cass Condors. In all kinds of weather, Gauntlett played perfectly.

Play after play, game after game, no matter how bad the weather, how wet, how cold his fingers were, Dave spiraled the pigskin to the right player at the right speed at the right location. One bad snap could have blown the perfect season. It would not take much for a ball to be snapped over the head of the quarterback, halfback or fullback, which could have resulted in a lost fumble or score by the opposing defense. Gauntlett was so valuable that Coach Pat did not use him on defense, like the rest of the team. He did not want to risk losing one of the keys to single wing success - a dependable, steadfast center. When the defense came onto the field it was usually just one player, Charlie Zurat, who played middle linebacker. So Gauntlett out, Zurat in. The rest of the guys played both ways.

Strangely enough, over 50 years later, at the former Maroon's Restaurant in Pottsville, PA, Dave spoke of his role on the team. Do you think he bragged about his amazing and consistent snaps? Or about the great blocks he made on much bigger guys? Nope. He remembered his one bad snap! In the championship game between Cass and Shamokin, in the rain, cold, and mud, Dave messed up a bit. Early in the game, he one-hopped the football to punter Ed "Gus" Gressik, who scooped it up like the baseball player he was, and booted it very deep into Shamokin territory. No harm! And Gus was the other secret weapon.

Gus Gressik, (actual game jersey below) who stood about 5 ft. 11 inches tall and weighed 185 pounds, lived with team captain, Russ Frantz. Gus was also the team co-captain. Not surprisingly, both had similar values, and "work ethics," if that is what it can be called in 16 year old boys. Gus also had the fine hands of a very good basketball and baseball player, which he was. He played varsity for four years. No doubt, he developed those nimble fingers and soft hands in other sports. Actually, Gus was Russ's nephew, or the son of Russ's sister, Gladys. In fact, they were born within six days of each other - a mom and her daughter both having a baby the same Christmas week in 1940! So, although he was the same age as Russ, he was actually *Uncle* Russ to Gus, his nephew.

Gressik was another unsung hero. Remember, no opponent scored the entire football season. This was in a large part due to field position, where many times, Cass' opponents started their offensive series deep on their own side of the 50-yd line, sometimes close to their goal line. This was very important to the team's success, as Gus punted the ball long, strong, and high. And by the time the opponents punt receiver caught the ball, the Cass team was there waiting to gang tackle him. Few punts were returned for more than a couple of yards when the mass of Cass hit the poor guy catching the ball. Usually more than a few flying bodies were involved.

Gus had a unique unorthodox approach to punting. After he caught Dave Gauntlett's nice spirals, he sort of hopped a quick two-stepper and - BOOM! Off went he ball over the oncoming players' heads. Unbelievably, Gus had no mishandled snaps or blocked punts the entire season. This was a tremendous advantage for Cass. They had a defense that was known for its toughness - they shut down runners and batted down or intercepted passes. And opposing teams most always started in poor field position, near the shadows of their own goal posts. Then the formidable Cass defense took over.

He didn't just punt. He was also a guard on Cass' solid defensive wall. Actually he was a triple threat, as he was also a solid blocker and a hard charging, pulling guard, part of the offensive blocking machine. Coach Pat, though he liked his single wing tricky offense, actually loved his defense even more. He once said to his offense, "Just don't screw it up, don't fumble, just let our defense get back on the field." And thanks to Gus' punts, that defense started deep in enemy territory, where they usually kept the other team's offense pinned. Sadly, at age 60, Gus died of a heart attack, while going for a walk on January 1, 2000. Ironically, this happened in Schuylkill Haven, PA, whose team Gus helped beat by a score of 40-0.

The third weapon was scout and unofficial (unpaid) coach John Pytko. John was a star for Cass High back in 1953. He had played solid football, baseball and basketball back then, and was still a pretty darn good athlete in 1957. He not only scouted opponents for Cass, but during the week he also ran the scout team during practice, simulating the quarterback of the upcoming team. He still had a good arm and threw some good balls downfield in practice to Frantz and Butsko among others.

Mike Kovich was another key to the success Cass experienced. Cass was known for its tough work in the trenches - the offensive and defensive lines. Mike was another unpaid assistant, and specialized in coaching the basics to the lineman - blocking and tackling. Single wing offense was complicated, and Mike taught the line their blocking assignments. Though Mike worked as a teacher at St. Clair High School, he seldom missed a Cass practice, and was well liked by all the Cass players. He also acted as the team trainer, and helped keep the guys in shape, and taped them up as needed.

Maybe the most important weapon was the entire **defense**. Cass employed a unique 4-5-2 setup, where four linemen always rushed. The five linebackers either rushed or covered someone sneaking out for a pass. But *any* of the five could rush, depending on the situation. Thus, the opponent's offense was constantly off guard. And the guys on defense knew each other so well that they played like mind-readers, anticipating the offensive plays. When the coin was tossed at the beginning of each game, the team co-captains, Frantz, Gressik, and Kachmar, always elected to kick off. This meant that Cass would start the game on defense, and planned to hold the opponent deep in their territory. Then after the opponent punted, their offense would come in, usually in decent field position.

Coach Pat practiced a form of psychological warfare. He added two inches and about 20 pounds to each player in the game program. For example, Ted Wannisky told me he was really 5 ft. 8 inches tall and weighed 160 pounds, but the program read "Wannisky, #11, QB, 5 ft. 10 inches,

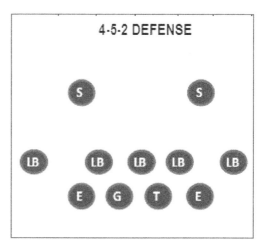

180 lbs." Thus, the legend of "big" Cass Township was enhanced.

The last and maybe the *best* of the secret weapons were the backup players. They were the supporting cast and were unselfish and humble to the core. Week in and week out, they were tough, and they were hit hard by the starters in practices. They hit back pretty well, too. This hard work kept the starters on their toes, and allowed the backups to learn the plays, too. They also got action in some games, and a few, like Ron Ney, played on Cass special teams. Every time Gus Gressik punted, Ney replaced him at the guard position. They mainly played supporting roles. There was not much glory in this, but as I mentioned earlier they were all about teamwork. They were great guys like Steve Yuschock, Mike Milyo, Rich Krasnitsky, Steve Pecovich, and Joe Witcofsky.

Chapter 5

Single Wing Formation Cass Style

Back in the early days of football, many teams - both high school and college - employed the so-called single wing formation. Supposedly, it was invented back in the early 1900s as Teddy Roosevelt supported legislation to make college football safer and end the many fatalities happening on the field. The madness in football played at that time included the "flying wedge," and other dangerous mass-momentum plays and kickoff returns.

The single wing and the forward pass were born in that era. Ironically, the great "Pop" Warner employed the single wing offense in Carlisle, PA, a mere 45 miles from the Cass coal region. Pop coached the *Indian School*, as it was called, from 1907 to 1914. He called the single wing the "Carlisle formation," as he was one of the first to employ it. Even the great Jim Thorpe played single wing under Coach Warner.

The single wing offense evolved over time as teams employed it to their advantage. Cass was one of those teams, and they executed it to near perfection. They did this as Coach ran plays in practice over and over and over - practicing, and running plays repeatedly until the guys could do it without thinking, a sort of *muscle memory*. They first walked through the play, without contact. Next they ran it at half speed, with Coach, in his animated way, gesturing and running the ball himself, showing the guys his version. Finally they executed the exact same play at full speed until every player memorized his role, and that of everyone else on the line and in the backfield.

Coach Pat's drills and repetition were just a small example of his inner fire, temper, and intensity. He yelled, spit and blew his whistle until they got it right. Single wing offense was simple yet complex; simple in that they ran straight dive plays, and handoffs. But complex, since the handoff could lead to reverses, reverse passes, fake reverses, and yes - even double reverses. Defenses were constantly kept off balance as Cass created illusions and ran the ball when it looked like a pass was coming - and passed when it seemed, smelled and appeared that a running play was imminent. Then the trickery and wizardry began with execution of the play.

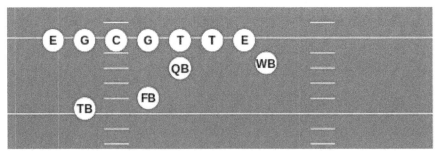

The basics were that the center snapped the ball under his legs to someone in the backfield, either the QB, halfback, or blocking back (fullback). Not knowing who got the ball thoroughly confused defenses. Separated from the other backs, split out near the tight end, was the wingback, or "single-wing" man, which gave the name to that offensive style. (see diagram)

A simplified version most football fans are familiar with is the shotgun offense where the quarterback receives the direct snap about five yards from the center. In this century, single wing made a comeback of sorts when the NFL Miami Dolphins employed what became known as the "Wildcat" offense. The Florida Gators used parts and pieces of it when former Heisman winner Tim Tebow either ran or threw a "jump pass." He beat the Oklahoma Sooners by a score of 24-14, and won the national college championship in 2009. Harry Heffron was the "Tim Tebow" jump passer for Cass.

Cass used power football with an *unbalanced* line, as part of the single wing magic. This meant instead of a center, with a guard, then a tackle, then an end (three guys on each side of the center), Cass had a center with four guys on one side, usually the right, and two on the other. Essentially, two tackles on the unbalanced side. And the best part: opponents never knew which side would be the strong one on a given play!

Two players, Harry Heffron and Tony Antonelli were actually ends in the 1956 football season, yet made the transition to offensive single wing backs in 1957. This is just one example of how these guys worked together, and played for the team - not the *me* or the *I* or for individual statistics. Team chemistry was as important as size and speed. That characteristic served Cass players well, both on the field and off, *for the rest of their lives.*

Fullback Frank Machita, who handled the ball a lot in single wing, reminds me of the great George Blanda, of Oakland Raider NFL fame: he would not only score the TD, but then would also kick the extra point. Frank sacrificed for the team, too. He went from a halfback to a blocking back or fullback in 1957, and cleared a path for the smaller faster guys. Guys like quarterbacks Ted Wannisky and Wash Brennan, and the unbelievable little man with the big heart - George Ryan, (5 ft. 5 inches, and only a junior, lucky #13, affectionately known as "Beakley").

So here is the secret sauce of Cass' single wing - *interchangeable backs.* Plus one extra guy to either run plays in or to give someone a break. A single wing backfield was composed of four backs - Cass had five to choose from for four positions. All got equal playing time. They were wingback, Weiner Antonelli; quarterback, Ted Wannisky (later Wash Brennan, who replaced Ted); halfback, Beakley Ryan; halfback, Harry Heffron; and fullback, Frank Machita. So with either Brennan or Wannisky in at quarterback, there was always a spare back on the sidelines. But if necessary, they could switch roles. This kept opposing defenses confused and off guard.

See? Coach Pat was the head mechanic with a lot of tools in the Cass toolbox. And these were well polished quality tools. Made in America! They just had to be employed at the right time and at the right field position.

The other undisclosed element to their opponents was that Coach Pat only had about 10 or so regular plays in the playbook! (Ok, there were some trick plays added from time to time, depending on the opponent.) Cass practiced the basic plays so many times during the week and during the off-season, that they perfected them. The linemen and backs knew where they needed to be, and what their duties were. It was all about timing. The linemen also were so skilled at their blocking assignments that they made it look easy. But it was not easy - it was like a well-rehearsed ballet where everyone knew the right moves. And everyone else's, too. And remember, Assistant Coach Mike Kovich rehearsed the line on their blocking assignments – over and over.

Chapter 6

First Game Rivalry

Game 1 (27-0) at Minersville
Friday, Sep 13, 1957

Yep. Friday the 13th of September. Go figure. Finally after all the late summer two-a-day practices, the sweat, and the intensity during workouts, the big day had arrived. Irishman, Mr. Thomas Mahoney was the long time Cass team bus driver. (His daughter Anna Mary would later marry a Cass player, Rich Krasnisky.) Mahoney was not intimated easily. When Pat was getting anxious and was trying to get Mr. Mahoney to hurry, Mahoney said in his Irish accent, "Bejeesus Pat, they won't be startin' without ya, now, will they?"

The loaded bus pulled out of the Cass High School lot and began the slow downhill, two-mile ride from Primrose to Minersville High School stadium. Only a few hours before, Coach had driven up the hill from his home on Laurel Street to Cass High. The team was trying to be calm, but everyone had butterflies in their stomachs. Cass had not beaten Minersville in years. In fact, Coach Pat was actually pretty excited, yet shared the players' anxiety. He not only lived in Minersville, but used to teach Chemistry and coach basketball at Minersville High prior to taking charge of all sports coaching duties for Cass in 1954. So you can imagine some of the strange thoughts rattling around in Coach's head.

The prior evening, Coach's entire street, including in front of his 315 Laurel Street home, was "white-washed" (a mixture of lime powder and water) with a lot of what we would now call graffiti. It was mostly friendly, but there were some shots such as, "Too bad you left M-ville to coach at Cass – you will lose!" And "Hey Coach, you won't score a point against us." They even painted "Traitor,"

"Loser," "Move to Cass." And one outspoken loser must have scrolled this one, "Cass, Cass - kiss my ass!" After a few heavy rainfalls, it all washed away.

The kids who painted that on the street had good reason to be brash. Cass had not beaten Minersville for six seasons. In 1951 Cass Coach Sandy Phillips used his star running back, Paul Gober, to beat Minersville by a score of 12 - 6.

Cass was so near Minersville that Cass agreed to play all their home games on Thursday nights, and Minersville played on Fridays, since they shared the same fan base. But to this day, it seems strange that Cass had school on the day after home games. In fact, Coach even had his team practice after school on Fridays. Plus, the adults and most fans had work on Fridays. Many had to get up very early in the morning for work in the coal mines and local factories. But not this opening night, since Minersville was the home team and Friday night football under the lights was the big show in town, and the stadium was full.

If co-captains Russ Frantz, Gus Gressik, Steve Kachmar, and the guys really had butterflies, they flew away pretty quickly. Minersville won the coin toss and Frank Machita kicked off to Minersville. The season had begun with tremendous tension and apprehension. The pressure eased quickly, as Cass scored two touchdowns in the very first period.

A football has a funny shape and can take some very odd bounces. Early in the game Gus punted his signature punt high into the cool night air. Minersville return man, Bob Clarke, mishandled that oblong shaped pigskin, and big Harry Butsko was right there to land on the ball. He cradled it at the Minersville 30-yd line. Now Cass had only 90 feet to score their first TD of the season. And four plays later, the "big time" underdog Cass offense did just that - they scored a touchdown.

Sometimes the football gods are fair; other times they seem to play cruel jokes at plays and weird happenings on the football field. This time it only seemed fair that Harry, who just recovered the muffed catch, caught a 13 yard pass from quarterback Ted Wannisky. And to really get the players, fans, and coach's adrenaline flowing, Frank Machita kicked the extra point to make it 7-0, only minutes into the game. (Wally Brennan was the holder - more on him later). In those days, there were no soccer-style kickers, and Frank met those footballs straight ahead from the tip of his toes. You may remember one of the last pro football kickers to kick this way - the great George Blanda.

There was silence in the stadium for a few minutes, and then the crowd got louder as Minersville received the kickoff and worked their way all the way down the field to within 18 yards of the Cass goal line. Minersville used their regular T-formation with quirks some called a "flying saucer offense." They had to be thinking, "OK here we go, we tie the game at 7-7, and put an end to these Cass guys' lucky touchdown." Cass put a stop to that plan and silenced the crowd with a 4th down stop. Few teams kicked field goals back then, so it was not unusual for a team like Minersville or Cass to go for the first down on 4th down.

Now Cass had the ball, but they were pinned deep in their own territory. Could the Minersville defense hold them there? Not exactly! On the very next play, Cass caught Minersville napping. With the help of a few nice blocks by Stevie Kachmar and Dave Gauntlett, Cass running back Tony "Weiner" Antonelli sprang into the clear and sprinted 82 yards for the Cass touchdown. There was not a Minersville player within 15 yards of Tony as he glided across the goal line. To say the crowd was shocked would be an understatement.

Now, could Frank make it 14-0? Nope, he missed this one, which works right into the story, as on Friday the 13th, the score was now 13-0. That proved to be enough to break Minersville's spirit when the Cass defensive gang tackled and kept the Battlin'

Miners pinned on their side of the midfield stripe for the rest of the first half. In fact, deep at their own 15-yd line, Minersville tried a pass and thanks to a great rush by Joe Hydock and Gus Gressik, the pass was picked off by someone in a Maroon Jersey with #18 on it, not the intended white jersey of Minersville. That would be the tough Harry Heffron, who intercepted the football and ran it back to where Minersville threw it from.

Harry was pumped, and wanted the ball. He got the call and ran the ball all the way to the Minersville 7-yd line. Now it was time for the little big man, George "Beakley" Ryan, to strut his stuff. So, on Friday the 13th, with the score 13-0, Cass jersey #13 got his chance, as Beakley headed around the right side. Beakley side-stepped and faked at least three Minersville defenders to lean his 5 ft 5 inch 145 pound solid frame into the end zone. *The Pottsville Republican*, Schuylkill County's leading newspaper referred to him as "diminutive." Indeed! His teammates said he played as if he were 6 feet tall. Ryan (no relation to Cass School Board president, Jimmy Ryan) was a proud, honest, humble, and fun kid who remained mischievous, well into fatherhood. No kicking the extra point, this time; Harry must have still been pumped up, as he ran the three yards for the extra point to make it a 20-0 lead for Cass. Both teams headed towards the small locker rooms beneath the junior high for their half-time break. One team was excited, the other in a state of pure shock - Minersville, the favored home team!

Anyone who has played sports knows that locker rooms can be strange places, and tend to take on the personality of the head coach. Half-time breaks are never the same. But this time and this place had to contain what can only be called emotional intensity. Coach Pat was pleased inside, but was careful not to smile, as he was a focused guy and did not want his players to get overconfident - ever. Remember, this was not only the very first game of the season, but it was between local rivals, and was being played on the home field of the highly favored Minersville "Battlin' Miners." Moreover, it was supposed to be a blowout, a glorious

Friday night romp by the Minersville boys against this thinly populated Cass High School that was just up the hill on Minersville's main street, Sunbury Street. But all the fans could mutter about as they walked under the stands to buy their hot chocolate for five cents were thoughts like, "How is it even possible that we are behind 20-0?" "What the hell is going on?" Or they said things like, "Don't worry, we'll come back and kill 'em in the second half." "Cass was just lucky, that's all." Maybe it was luck, or maybe there was more to this *lucky* start than anyone could know. At this point, no one could realize that fate and destiny also would manifest throughout the season. Or could it be that Cass was just a great collection of the right athletes at the right time and the right place with just the right coach?

In the Minersville locker room, Coach Harold Stefl tore into guys like Joe Willinsky, who would later become Minersville's Chief of Police. He could not believe his players like Harry Close, Ron Murphy, Martin, Mashack, Burinsky, Ray Polinsky, and Ted Malewicz were being physically manhandled by Cass both on offense and defense. The visiting team locker room in Minersville was right next door to the home team, and you could actually hear some voices through the old wooden walls. Coach Pat continued to be "cautiously proud" of the team, but was hard at work on the chalkboard making adjustments with his "X"s and "O"s, representing each position. He broke the chalk more than once because he was so animated.

Meanwhile assistant coaches Pytko and Kovich re-taped the guys' ankles and uniforms, while Coach Pat asked his team captain, Russ Frantz, what was working and what was not. Pat had a tradition he followed in all the schools he coached: he bought two dozen oranges at the Minersville A&P store on the way to each game and personally handed them out, cut into quarters. Funny, but he was a creature of habit; he coached at four different high schools in his career, and always stopped in the exact same grocery store at the bottom of Sunbury Street. Everyone in small towns seems to know everyone else, so it was not unusual for the locals to say, "Good luck, Coach," or "Go get 'em Pat."

The Minersville comeback was apparently not meant to be. In fact, neither team scored in the third period, in large part thanks to the strong Cass defense keeping the Miners pinned deep in their own territory. Both defenses proved themselves worthy, as Cass tried in vain to continue pounding the Miners. Harry Heffron took the opening kickoff almost to midfield, where he was gang tackled. If there had been highlight films in those days, the next play would have been one. A few plays later, quarterback, Ted Wannisky threw a beautiful pass to Harry Butsko, who made an amazing leaping catch, and took the ball 26 yards all the way to the Minersville 20-yd line, known as the "red-zone" today. The way the game was going, you would think Cass would drive to ice the game and coast to victory, but not so! The Miners stopped them four plays later after only two yards were gained.

Maybe it was the Miners turn to start their comeback? The packed house sure hoped so, as they cheered wildly. The cheers turned to "Ahhhs" when on the very first play Cass' Charlie Zurat intercepted the ball at almost the same place Minersville held Cass on the previous series - right near the 20-yd line. However, a penalty was called on Cass after the interception, and Cass began the series about 30 yards from pay dirt. Once again Cass' offense could not move against the stubborn Miners and Minersville took over again - this time at their own 30 yard line. Remember it was still only Cass 20 to Minersville's zero, but in football, it seems there is always hope for turnarounds and comebacks.

And that is exactly how it looked when Minersville quarterback Kopich threw a long pass to Rodnick who ran it all the way to the Cass 35-yd line. Another highlight play, since the ball touched two Cass players' hands before Rodrick pulled it in. Once again, the Miners fans and players were excited as this could be the comeback they so desperately needed and wanted. Could the Miners score here and get back into the ballgame? Not exactly.

They fumbled and Cass' Harry Heffron was working his magic on defense and grabbed the fumble right at the 35-yd line. Hope died for Minersville on this play, as Cass drove the ball methodically into Minersville territory, with some great single wing basic running and passing. George Ryan made a few good runs, as did Harry Heffron and Tony Antonelli, working overtime.

Now it was time to call a play for Russ Frantz. Quarterback Ted Wannisky threw a beautiful pass about 23 yards and Frantz pulled it in right on cue. He scored his first touchdown of his senior year as he trotted into the end zone. Frank kicked this extra point, and that was the beginning of the Perfect Season: Cass 27, Minersville 0. Now it was time for the players to hurry onto the bus and get out of the small confines underneath the metal stands of Minersville's stadium. A few of the Minersville fans, mostly high school kids, threw stones and eggs at the bus. Coach Pat gave the order, "Put your helmets on and let's get the hell out of here!" They laughed, joked, and relived game moments all the way back up the hill about two miles to the safety of their own high school. A short ride, but what a ride that must have been!

Thus began the quest for the holy grail of American football: to win all games and hold opponents to zero points – a perfect

season! At this point in the season, of course, no one dared think they were on that quest, even after a near-perfect ball game!

In honor of this victory, James ("Jimmy") V. Ryan, President of the Cass Township School Board declared the following Monday a school holiday for Cass students, faculty, and players.

Chapter 7
The Beat Goes On

Game 2 (32-0) at Nescopeck
Saturday, September 21, 1957

A week and a day later, Cass played another road game. It was an unusually hot fall Saturday. The players had to get up early that Saturday morning and be at Cass Township High School by 9 AM. Coach Pat held a short practice after school on the Friday before the Saturday game. He *warned* the team to "Get to bed no later than 10 o'clock." A very hot day. They rode the un-air-conditioned school bus from Schuylkill County to Luzerne County, almost 50 miles away. There was no Interstate 81, so they had to travel the back roads. The bus driver, Mr. Mahoney, left the windows open. He had to navigate through small towns - Ashland, Centralia, Ringtown, and Nuremburg. The players were warm and sweaty, as they had most of their uniforms on already. There were no locker rooms at Nescopeck. An hour and a half later they arrived – soaked in sweat.

Cass proved the season opener was no fluke. This time the Condors beat underdog Nescopeck by a score of 32-0. The guys claim it was over 90 degrees, as they remember the Hershey bars melting. There were no water bottles, no Gatorade, no sports drinks, just a five gallon metal bucket filled with water and a metal dipper which the players all shared. Coach Pat used to yell at the guys, "Hey, don't drink over the water bucket!"

Because it was so far away and on a Saturday, there is not much written about this game in any of the newspapers I researched. And the guys remember only so much. This is a short but powerful chapter, for Cass that is.

Frank Machita ran strong against Nescopeck and scored a 20 yard touchdown early in the first period. He kicked the extra point, so Cass only had a lead of 7-0 at halftime. This was a great half for

Nescopeck Township, as they were also a small high school like Cass. Only about 50 students in their senior class, not exactly a football powerhouse. Just as Cass was absorbed by Minersville, several years after the 1957 season, Nescopeck also became a part of another school - Berwick. The Cass players reportedly called the other team the *Nesco-peckers* that day as they bantered.

The miserable heat took its toll. Both teams seemed exhausted in the second period, and they were unable to score. They traded punts a few times.

As you may imagine, Coach Pat was not a happy camper at halftime. He wondered what happened to his mighty team that upset Minersville 27-0 a week earlier. Pat yelled at them, huddled under the shade of an oak tree (There were no locker rooms). "What are you guys, a bunch of PANSIES? Are you going to play some football?" Not exactly a Knute Rockne style 1928 rousing speech like "Win one for the Gipper," but I guess it got the guys' attention. They went out and scored *four* touchdowns in the second half.

The perfect season was almost derailed that hot and humid afternoon. Cass Ron Ney's second half kickoff was returned by a Nescopeck player for what seemed to be a touchdown. Cass breathed a sigh of relief as soon as they saw the flag. An alert official thankfully threw the penalty flag (a Nescopeck player stepped out of bounds) and the touchdown was called back. Cass held Nescopeck and they had to punt.

Now the Cass Condors had the ball and the momentum. After some single wing basics a few plays later, Weiner Antonelli scored from the 4-yd line. This time he only had to fight a few yards to the goal line - no 82 yard dash on this hot day like he did in the prior game at Minersville. Frank Machita missed the point attempt so the score was 13-0.

Nescopeck's day was over. They had to punt again after three plays and now the Cass offense was on a roll. They meticulously moved the ball downfield, racking up a few first downs. Ball control. Frank Machita was hot that day, as he scored his second touchdown, this time from the 9-yd line. And he stayed in for the extra point, kicking it up and through the goalposts. Now the score was 20-0.

Russ Frantz remembers the 4th quarter well. He should; he caught two touchdown passes. The first one was a nice long pass from Ted Wannisky for about 40 yards. Frantz sprinted to the end zone untouched. One of the Cass backs threw a missed pass and the extra point failed. Cass 26-0.

Nescopeck had a bad day. After another three and out, they punted to Cass. Cass again drove downfield with strong runs by Beakley Ryan, Weiner Antonelli, and Frank Machita. After nothing but ground gains, the Nescopeck defense was looking for another run from the 3-yd line. That is why Ted Wannisky called for a direct snap, where he faked a run. He stopped at his strong offensive line somewhere behind Tony Phillips and Joe Hydock. He jumped straight up and threw a classic jump pass to Russ Frantz for six points.

Now the Condors thought they had Nescopeck napping so they tried the exact same play for the extra point. It did not work. The final score was Cass 32-0.

Ted Wannisky had the best game of his football career that sizzling day. He threw two touchdown passes to Russ Frantz and two to Frank Machita. (He would only play for three more games until one fateful day on October 10th, 1957, when he broke his collarbone). And Weiner Antonelli began his scoring streak: two consecutive games. The shutout was now in its infancy but still intact at two games.

Chapter 8

First Home Game

Game 3 (34-0) at Home vs. West Mahanoy Township
Thursday, Sep 26, 1957

A mere five days after the Saturday game, Cass played its third game of the season - their home debut and one to be remembered! The local fans were pretty fired up by now. Cass had scored a total of almost 60 points in its first two road games and the fans were now expecting more of the same. They would not be disappointed! After the first two shutout games, the buzz around the county had begun about the Cass football team and their great defense. Schuylkill County's Newspaper, *The Pottsville Republican*, sent sports reporter, Ronnie Christ, and a photographer to cover this Thursday night game. According to Mr. Christ, over 1,000 fans were there to see the Condors rout the West Mahanoy Township

Rams 34-0.

Harry Heffron scored twice. He told me he carried the ball so much, that he "wanted to let some of the other guys share in the fun!" He did not mind as he was a ferocious blocker, and he really loved that physical aspect of the game. Tony Antonelli kept his streak alive, and also ran for a touchdown. He now had scored in three consecutive games. Quarterback Ted Wannisky and Whitey Sinko each ran in for their first touchdown of the season.

That makes 93 points in three games which is a pretty prolific *offense* for a team known mostly for its great "no scoring allowed here" defense!

But let's take a step back to the first quarter of the game where no one scored. This was Cass' first home game and the fans wanted to see some action, especially since most people could not afford to attend away games. The previous week, West Mahanoy had been humiliated by St Clair 46-0, so with a scoreless quarter against Cass, they had to be feeling proud and ready to upset the Condors!

Here is where something numerically eerie occurs, something that has never been discussed or pointed out in the Cass sports stories. You already know the ending of this book, so surely you must be aware that Cass was UNSCORED UPON. In this, only the third game of the season, it should be obvious that I am not giving up any secrets. Hard-core Cass fans already know how Cass won the playoff game and they know the final score (2-0). They also know who famously blocked that punt for a safety, which happened more than two months after this game. It was Joe Hydock. And guess who scores in this, so far, scoreless game - Joe Hydock! And how, you ask? Of course, he scored the same way he did in the future, a safety, naturally.

This is how it happened. During the first half Cass' offense had the football and drove it all the way to the Rams' 3-yd line, and appeared ready to score. On first down at the 3-yd line they tried another running play: that is how they moved all the way down the field. No passes. Cass ran but fumbled the ball right at the goal line, and the Rams recovered! Coach Pat, known for his emotional, fiery approach to coaching had to be furious at that moment in time. The Cass defense smelled blood when Coach yelled a simple "GET EM now!" and Cass kept the Rams pinned at their own 1-yd line. On the very next play a fired up Joe Hydock slammed down a Rams ball carrier behind the goal line for a safety. Yes, the scoreboard read **Cass 2, West Mahanoy 0**, the same as it would read seven games later (2-0) thanks to Joe Hydock! Pat's anger instantly disappeared as his defense came through - again!

Remember, Harry Heffron scored twice in this game. Once in each half. Guess how Cass set up Harry's touchdown? The answer: defense, of course. Here is how Cass did it: After the safety West Mahanoy had to kick off to Cass: so now Cass is officially on offense. And just as their offense had fumbled on the goal line, it happened again! After the Rams started on their own 40-yd line, Cass' defense pushed them deep inside their own territory to force a 4th down punt. And in typical Cass defensive style, they rushed hard to partially block the punt and took over only 35 yards from their goal line. After a few running plays, Cass had the ball near their 20-yd line, a good time to call for a pass. Coach Pat always liked his trick plays. He coached his team captains to think "sideways" and not do what the defense was looking for.

Harry Heffron took the direct snap from Dave Gauntlett and scrambled to his right. He faked a pass, with his classic jump-pass style, but held on to the ball. He ran it all the way across the goal line for his first touchdown of the game. After Machita kicked it through the uprights for the extra point, the score was 9-0.

With the halftime score only Cass 9, West Mahanoy 0, what was going on with another slow first half for the Cass Condors? Remember, they fumbled a few times, and missed some real chances to knock the Rams out of the game. Coach Pat had to be a bit worried, but no "Pansies" speech this time since Cass was in its own familiar home-town locker room. He saw that West Mahanoy Township had played tough in the first half, so he knew he had to calm his boys down. He must have jump-started something, as Cass rallied in front of the home crowd and scored an amazing four touchdowns in the second half. FOUR.

In football when things are shaky, it is always good to get some momentum going, and Cass received the second half kickoff. The right guy received the kickoff, as Frank Machita got his chance and ran all the way to midfield. At this point, the Cass fans were getting pretty excited and were ready to put the game on ice. However, a few plays later, another Cass fumble kept the Rams' hope alive. Except for one thing called Cass **defense:** they held and forced West Mahanoy to punt on 4th down. After driving down the field all the way to the 18-yd line, Harry Heffron put a stake in the Rams heart. He raced along the sidelines to score his second touchdown of the game. Machita made it 16-0. It was all over now for West Mahanoy Township.

Joe Hydock was responsible for a safety and two points for Cass. He was not done with his own highlight reel performance: he intercepted a Rams pass to set up the next Cass score. That score did not take very long. On the next play, Antonelli, as the single wing back, took the ball right up the middle and bullied his way 23 yards right into the end zone. Amazing blocks by Tony Phillips and Joe Hydock opened up the hole for him, and Antonelli did the rest on his own. This made the score 22-0.

After the Rams got desperate and threw some air balls, Harry Butsko picked off a pass and ran it all the way inside the 20-yd line before the Rams pulled him down. Senior quarterback, Ted Wannisky called his own number and scored this time, making the game officially a blowout at 28-0.

Coach Pat knew they could not lose, but cautioned his defense not to let their guard down. He kept his starting defense in the game to preserve the shutout, but had no problem giving the substitutes a chance to play on offense. Sinko came in on offense and scored on the next series. The game mercifully ended 34-0.

The Cass home fans were overjoyed and were confident that everything they had heard about Cass was real. The momentum was building, as they had just witnessed the first of what would be five home shutouts. Cass had now won three in a row, and the Rams lost three in a row. This would be the last year West Mahanoy Township would field its own football team, as they merged with Mahanoy Township the next season. In an ironic twist of fate, it is likely that some of the juniors on the Rams team played with the Mahoney Township team the next season, 1958, the only team to score against the Cass Condors in two seasons.

Chapter 9

High Score

Game 4 (40-0) at Home vs. Schuylkill Haven
Thursday, Oct 3, 1957

The second home game of the season turned into a one-sided, old fashioned *drubbing*. There was no let-up, no first half parity and no leniency. The game was so one-sided, it ranked as the highest score in the 15 year history the two schools had played each other: 40-0! This would be the most points in a game Cass scored the remainder of the '57 football season. The underclassmen would go on to score more than 40 points twice the next season, but that special night, Cass embarrassed the Schuylkill Haven Hurricanes. Thanks to the hard-hitting, dominant defense, and the leg of

punter Gus Gressik, almost the entire game was played on the Hurricanes side of the 50 yard line.

Gus did something he never did before and would never do again in his football career: he scored a touchdown! In the 4th quarter with Cass leading 33-0, defensive guard, Gus Gressik, who wore Cass jersey #22, intercepted a Hurricane pass and ran it about 30 yards for the final score of the game. This game was probably the best example of how the Cass defense and offense worked in tandem, as their defense shut down the Hurricanes (only three first downs and a combined 86 yards of offense), and the Condors offense racked up an astonishing six touchdowns, which involved rushing for 199 yards and passing for 97, almost 300 yards of textbook single-wing offensive power and teamwork.

The players who scored touchdowns got the credit and accolades from the press, but the team knew the real heroes were the hard hitters who played offensive and defensive line: tackles, Joe Hydock and Tony Phillips; guards, Steve Yuschock, Charlie Zurat (on defense), Steve Kachmar, Gus Gressik, ; and center Dave Gauntlett.

Sophomore Walter "Wash" (or Wally) Brennan even got a chance to play quarterback, and give Ted Wannisky a well-deserved break. Brennan threw the first touchdown pass of his varsity career. In the 4th quarter, the sophomore threw a 22 yard pass to junior Beakley Ryan. The second smallest guy on the team had thrown a TD pass to the smallest player on the Cass squad, something they would repeat many more times in their playing days. They both also played together for the rest of the '57 year and again during the implausible continued UNSCORED upon run into the '58 season the next Fall.

The first score of the game came from a pass from Harry Heffron to Russ Frantz for a 35 yard touchdown. Harry said that in this game he ran for more first downs than any other football game he played in, but did not score in it. Harry later told me that he listened to the WPPA (a Pottsville, PA radio station), re-broadcast later. He heard local legend Ed Romance describe a specific play, his jump pass to Russ like this: "Heffron jumped up! He jumped down! It is complete to Russ Frantz. Touchdown!" Over 50 years later, he and Russ Frantz were still chuckling over this and trying to figure out how one indeed jumps *down*!

Other highlights included Charlie Zurat intercepting a pass late in the first half to set up Ted Wannisky's second touchdown pass of the game. Wannisky lobbed a 12 yard strike to a leaping Russ Frantz, his second scoring catch and run of the ballgame. Ted's first touchdown pass was a great pass to Harry Butsko from the 22-yd line.

In the second half, hard hitting fullback, Frank Machita rumbled for a seven yard touchdown. Charlie Zurat was a pure defensive specialist, a prototype linebacker. He was tough and fearless and seemed to thrive on the physical aspects of playing the game. He did not normally play offense: the team saved his strength to be the tough guy on defense.

Cass, not known for prolific offense, had now scored a staggering 133 points in four games, or an average of over 33 points a game, and held all four victims scoreless. On a sad note, Harry Butsko's father passed away the same week, and the guys dedicated the game to Harry's family.

According to *The Pottsville Republican* newspaper, Wannisky said the Condors knew they had something "special" after the Schuylkill Haven win. "Paul Zmuida was a Haven player, and his dad worked with my dad at Alcoa," (an aluminum processing plant in nearby Cressona, Pa), Wannisky said. "As we started winning games," his dad kept saying '"wait until you play Haven." Guess Paul's father was not a good fortune-teller or lottery player!

In a strange twist of fate, just two short years later, Coach Pat would not be the head coach of Cass anymore, but would become the coach of the team he had just routed - Schuylkill Haven.

Chapter 10

Loss of Senior QB

Game 5 (19-0) at Home vs. Ashland
Thursday, Oct 10, 1957

At the home field for the third week in a row, Cass was indeed on a roll, but the guys on the team remained humble and just enjoyed playing the game for the pure pleasure of it. There was no talk of scoreless seasons, records, or future fame. However, the Ashland "Black Diamonds" had only won one game so far and really wanted this one badly. Their coach and players knew this would be one night to remember if they could just upset undefeated Cass Township. What a skirmish it was, as the first quarter was a battle fought in the trenches of the offensive and defensive line. Linemen like Cass' Joe Hydock, Steve Kachmar, Steve Yuschock, Tony Phillips, Charlie Zurat and Gus Gressik played their hearts out but were stymied by the boys from nearby Ashland. This was a textbook display of some serious hard blocking and tackling by both sides. Harry Heffron, who would later be thrown out of this game for un-sportsman like conduct, claimed the boys from Ashland played tough but dirty. "They grabbed and poked in places they shouldn't have," he later told me.

Cass had its opportunities. On the very first play of the game an Ashland player muffed the kickoff, and big Harry Butsko recovered Cass' kickoff on about the Ashland 35-yd line. The momentum was short-lived when Cass was stymied and did not score. Even diehard Cass fans were a bit worried, as the Condors could not even get their passing game in gear. When the first quarter ended 0-0, Ashland had intercepted Cass passes twice. But, as mentioned, the linemen held each other at bay. Neither team was able to capitalize on any opportunity. During the quarter, Ashland punted and Cass was forced to start at its own 10-yd line. Remember, this was a strange place for them: they usually played on the other side of the 50-yd line, not deep in their territory! To add insult to injury, when Ryan passed the ball from this dangerous place, Ashland's Lew Kauffman intercepted him on about the Cass 30-yd line. Now the small stadium full of Cass fans cheered louder than ever for the defense to hold. Here is the kind of situation where Cass earned its gold-plated defensive reputation and somehow stopped Ashland in their tracks.

Two memorable things occurred in the second quarter, one good and one bad. The good thing was that Cass finally broke the scoring deadlock thanks to the hard-blocking offensive line and the great running ability of George "Beakley" Ryan. Ashland drove all the way to about the 30-yd line, and it looked a bit scary for Cass' scoreless season again. But the defense stiffened, as they say, and Cass stopped the Black Diamonds on 4th down. Now, thanks to the hard blocking mentioned above, Beakley literally took advantage of any small holes created, and did the rest on his own. He seemed to defy gravity and stayed on his feet play after play as Cass drove all the way to Ashland's 4-yd line. When they huddled up after the first down, there was only one guy whose number just had to be called - the #13 of Beakley, of course. He did not disappoint and powered his way into the end zone behind some nifty blocking by the likes of Gus Gressik and fullback Frank Machita. Frank was in good form that October night and kicked the extra point straight and true. The holder was sophomore Wash Brennan, who also played back-up quarterback (he already threw a touchdown pass against Schuylkill Haven) which now became a significant part of the story.

And the bad thing? It ended the season for an important ball handler for Cass. Signal caller Ted Wannisky would execute the last play of his life on a football field during the second quarter of the game. During the next series of plays, Ted was hurt and had to come out of the game. He broke his collarbone while blocking for George Ryan. Assistant Coach Mike Kovich and Coach Pat probably knew it was bad, but all that was known to the Cass fans and Pottsville reporter Ronnie Christ was that Wannisky suffered a "shoulder injury." Into the huddle comes 10th grader, Brennan, who would now start the rest of the season (also his junior and senior years). The guys in the huddle must have been a bit worried.

Imagine the feelings of the players as UNDEFEATED UNSCORED UPON Cass has only a slim 7-0 lead going into halftime, and they had just lost their experienced first string senior quarterback! Remember that hot Saturday back in September at Nescopeck when Cass also only led by that exact score, 7-0? That was the game where Coach Pat challenged his guys by calling them "pansies" at halftime. This time there was only an eerie silence around the stadium and the locker room - at first. This time the season was "maturing" and a lot of pride was at stake. If Cass could just hold Ashland scoreless they would have five wins and no losses and remain on top of the division.

Despite the low score, the players were not rattled. Coach Pat complimented the strong offensive and defensive line-play and stressed how they needed to keep wearing down Ashland. The players knew this, and they also knew they were bigger and stronger: by now, they expected more of themselves. They supported and encouraged each other to step up and play like they practiced - hard. They also were painfully aware that, without Ted, replacement Wash Brennan was under tremendous pressure and would likely be more than a bit nervous in the second half. This was a pivotal moment in the season, and the players had to rise to the challenge.

Ashland had to be fired up and proud of its performance in the first half. They held their own against Cass and did not look like a team that had only won one game so far that season. Being down by only one touchdown had to feel pretty good to the Black Diamonds' players and coaches. The coaches likely encouraged them to keep playing the same way, only harder and better.

Cass took the second half kickoff and mounted a drive all the way to the Ashland 37-yd line. Ashland was not about to give up and stopped Cass right there on third down. Facing a 4th down and about 5 yards, Coach Pat called for a punt, knowing that Gus could punt the ball out of bounds near the goal line. Coach also trusted his defense. Gressik did not disappoint his teammates and fans as he kicked the football out of bounds right at about the 10-yd line, where Ashland took over in the shadow of its own goal post.

Ashland tried to work the ball methodically out of the danger zone, but the Cass defensive line conjured up the magic they needed. This time it was Tony Phillips who rose to the occasion, as he nailed the Ashland quarterback before he knew what hit him. He recovered the football at about the 30-yd line. The Cass offense had a good chance to score and take control of this close game. But Coach Pat liked to catch the opposing teams off guard, and he must have figured Ashland would not expect the Cass backup quarterback to attempt a pass at this place and time on the field.

After a snap from Dave Gauntlett to Harry Heffron, Heffron handed it off to Wally, who dropped back to pass. Though both ends, Frantz and Butsko worked free, Wally was scrambling for his life; he probably was a bit scared to pass and maybe put a ball up for grabs. Somehow he broke free and looked like he just might score, but he was forced out of bounds only 15 yards from the goal line. During this play, the third period ended, and Cass still led by only 7-0. Now, with a fresh set of downs, it looked like Cass could surely score from here. But remember, the theme of this game seemed to be tough battles that were fought in the trenches. Somehow, some way, Ashland dug in and fought off the hard blocks of Cass and held them for four straight plays and Ashland actually took over at their own 10-yd line.

The 4th quarter was "Cass time," the best time to wear down their opponent. This was where the long practices and the tough conditioning paid off. It was Cass' routine to play in enemy territory and that is exactly the script they followed the rest of the game. After some more see-saw action, Harry Heffron scored from the 2-yd line, head down, bowling his way over a few defenders. Frank missed this extra point so it was now 13-0, which seemed to be a lucky number for Cass and Ryan's jersey number too! Now there would be no stopping Cass, as they regained both momentum and field position during the rest of the 4th quarter. The Condors kept the ball in play on Ashland's side of the 50-yd line, their comfort zone.

It was Tony Antonelli's turn to shine. He scored the next touchdown, from the 2-yd line, the same place where Harry previously hit pay dirt. He had now scored in four of the five games, ironically having had his streak broken in only the high scoring Schuylkill Haven blowout. The score was now 19-0. The extra point was missed, but irrelevant, as this is where the game ended. Neither Ashland nor Cass for that matter, had anything left to give.

(Frank Machita, #20, with the ball, Whitey Sinko, #12, blocking against Ashland – same team - but in 1958. The picture is too cool to *not* include in this 1957 write-up.)

Pittston Gazette

PITTSTON, PA., THURSDAY, OCTOBER 17, 1957

75c DELIVERS
The Gazette to Your Home for 1 Month
Just Phone OL 4-3311

108th Year

TEN PAGES

FLU OR GRIPPE HAS EFFECT LOCAL SCHOOLS, TWO CLOSED

Royal Welcome For Elizabeth Nation's Capital Led By Ike

SICKNESS SPREADING STATEWIDE

PITTSTON AND WEST SIDE CLOSE

FLU CLAIMED 30 LIVES IN US THIS WEEK

By GAY PAULEY
(United Press Correspondent)

William A. Clark, Retired Major Of State Police, Dies

FLOWERS FOR THE QUEEN

MRS. WILLIAM A. CLARK

Simpson Sees Need For Tax Cut, Notes High Defense Costs

By VINCENT J. BURLEY
United Press Staff Correspondent
Washington, Oct. 17 —

Scout Rally At Pittston High On Monday, Nov. 4th

Summations In Meeker Trial

30-Day-Weather Outlook Nation

Washington, Oct. 17 —

BARBS

A LOT OF LAW

Radio Repairs
Strub's Radio Shop

Chapter 11

Flu Postponed the Game

Game 6 at Home vs. Blythe Township postponed due to flu Thursday Oct 17, 1957

A serious flu hit Blythe in October 1957. Both Cass and Blythe Township agreed to reschedule this home game for Cass, as too many of their players finally succumbed to the flu. Of great significance, other county schools had already postponed games for the same reason; they did not have enough healthy players to even field a team. This came back to haunt Cass statistically, as some teams never made up their missed games. This affected the end of season standings in a complex way. What a lot of folks did not realize is that this was not a coal region, Schuylkill County or state of Pennsylvania localized event, but one that affected the entire world population. This flu epidemic or *influenza pandemic* was very serious indeed, as almost 70,000 people died in the U.S., and it claimed well over *one million lives* worldwide. Less than 100 miles away in Valley Forge, Pennsylvania, a mid-July Boy Scout Jamboree of more than 53,000 kids was probably a catalyst in spreading the flu in Pennsylvania.

This was actually the "Asian Flu" outbreak of influenza virus "A." Most experts claim that it originated in China in early 1956 and lasted until 1958. If it were not for a vaccine developed in 1957 that contained the outbreak, no doubt, the death toll would have been far, far worse. According to *globalsecurity.org,* "The virus came to the U.S. quietly, with a series of small outbreaks over the summer of 1957. When U.S. children went back to school in the fall, they spread the disease in classrooms and brought it home to their families. Infection rates were highest among school children, young adults, and pregnant women in October 1957. Most influenza and pneumonia-related deaths occurred between September 1957 and March 1958. The elderly had the highest rates of death."

According to the *Center for Biological Security,* "The 1957-58 pandemic was such a rapidly spreading disease that it became quickly apparent to U.S. health officials that efforts to stop or slow its spread were futile. Thus, no efforts were made to quarantine individuals or groups, and a deliberate decision was made not to cancel or postpone large meetings such as conferences, church gatherings, or athletic events for the purpose of reducing transmission. No attempt was made to limit travel or to otherwise screen travelers. Emphasis was placed on providing medical care to those who were afflicted and on sustaining the continued functioning of community and health services. The febrile, respiratory illness brought large numbers of patients to clinics, doctors' offices, and emergency rooms, but a relatively small percentage of those infected required hospitalization."

Some local schools like Lansford and Summit Hill had to cancel games due to sick players. This would come back to haunt Cass in the final standings. I explain the reasons later in Chapter 16, Championship Controversy.

Chapter 12

Monday Night High School Football

Game 6 (35-0) at Home vs. Blythe Township
Monday, Oct 21, 1957 (Make-up game)

Many years before NFL Monday Night Football, Cass played "Monday Night High School Football." Both school officials agreed to play the game postponed from the previous Thursday. This is an interesting bit of trivia, as now Cass played on a Thursday (several games), a Friday, a Saturday, and now a Monday evening. Only a "sparse throng" attended this weeknight offensive spectacle, according to *The Pottsville Republican.*

The Blythe "Black Panthers" showed up ready to win their first ballgame. By now, Cass had a bull's eye on their helmets, as teams rose above their normal level of play to take on the undefeated Condors. Blythe still had two players down with the flu: quarterback, Nelson Breisch and tackle, Joe Strauss. One of Cass' greatest advantages was its toughness, due in part to the hard practices, conditioning, and their tough heritage. So Cass was ready to go with two exceptions: Harry Heffron was out with the flu; and by now, it was officially known that Ted Wannisky was out for the rest of the season with a broken collarbone. That meant 10th grader Wally Brennan got his first start of the season and was the single wing quarterback. Fans, coaches and players, wondered if he would rise to the occasion or buckle under the scrutiny and the pressure.

Another ever-present danger to a winning team like Cass was letting down its guard, taking an opponent too lightly. But after their last game where they only led by 7-0 going into the last quarter, they were well prepared, both mentally and physically. Apparently, they were in no mood for a repeat of that type of close game scenario. The mighty Condors cranked out four touchdowns in the first half. The defense was again nothing short of spectacular: they never allowed the Panthers past their own 45-yd line.

Multi-talented Frank Machita had not scored a single point lately. He had not been in the end zone since he scored twice against Nescopeck on Sep 21st, exactly a month earlier and once against Schuylkill Haven in the 40-0 contest on October 3rd. Frank was ready to do more than just block or kick extra points on that Monday evening. Early in the first quarter, he followed a nice block by Joe Hydock and did the rest himself: he plowed in from about 10 yards to score the first touchdown. No kicking extra points on this night. Frank ran the extra point himself for a 7-0 lead, which is how the first quarter ended.

The line blocked like champs, and after some great runs by Frank Machita, George Ryan, and Weiner Antonelli, Cass was again on the 10-yd line. Now the dam burst loose, as "rookie" Wally Brennan played like a veteran and threw a perfect 10 yard pass to Russ Frantz: Russ used his 6 ft. 3 inch height and basketball leaping ability to pull in the football with a Blythe defender on his back. Machita again ran the extra point to make it 14-0. On the Panthers next possession, big Joe Hydock alertly used his 205 pounds to run over the Panthers and recover a football on about the Cass 40-yd line. A few plays later from the 14-yd line, Beakley Ryan took the direct snap and got into his passing stance. He found Russ Frantz, who made a great catch in full stride and raced across the goal line for his second touchdown. With the single wing, would Machita again run in the extra point? Not this time, as Beakley did the honors plunging in for the extra point. After two scores, Frantz got some rest, and back up, Rich Krasnitsky got a bit of playing time at end in this game.

After a short possession by the Panthers, Cass scored again. This time Coach Pat reached into his single wing bag of tricks and called a *triple* reverse. After two handoffs, Tony Antonelli ended up with the pigskin and performed the final leg of the triple reverse to score. Machita made it 21-0 running for his second extra point of the game.

Time was running out in the first half, with the Panthers in possession, back deep (again) in their own territory. Remember the trepidation Wash Brennan may have had as the starting quarterback? Well, in these days most players played offense and defense, and Wally did not get a break here. He performed double duty as a safety, since he also had to take Ted Wannisky's defensive position. If he had not earned the veterans' respect yet, he did it on the very next play. He intercepted Panthers quarterback Schneider's pass inside of the 40-yd line and took it all the way into the end zone for his first running score of the season. With the extra point by Machita, it was now 28-0. Cass ended the first half on top of the world.

Time for Blythe to pack it in and go home? No way. In the 2nd half, the Black Panthers defense stiffened and only allowed Cass one more touchdown. But it was their offense that could have ruined Cass scoreless season. Blythe was moving the ball nicely in the 3rd quarter. They crossed midfield, made a few first downs and drove all the way into Cass territory. They were only about 35 yards from the goal line. Remember the fullback on offense named Machita who already notched a touchdown? Now Frank Machita was linebacker Machita, and it seems he had enough of Blythe pushing Cass around.

Machita somehow took the ball away from Blythe's quarterback, Frank Schneider, as he was trying to cut into the Cass defense. Cass took over on the 35-yd line. The scare was over. Now it was the Condors turn to make some first downs and move the ball downfield in the other direction. The single wing offense executed the same plays they always did - direct snaps to Machita, Ryan, and Brennan. A few handoffs to Antonelli, but nothing too fancy. They drove for 14 straight plays all the way to the 1-yd line. They also bled off the rest of the time left in the 3rd quarter.

Now it was Beakley's turn. He had already thrown a touchdown pass earlier, so why not run one in? He simply plowed straight ahead through a nice hole made by Steve Kachmar and Dave Gauntlett and scored to make it 34-0. Ryan came out of the lineup and was replaced by Mike Milyo: he made the extra point, his only score of the season. Milyo was now on the board as a player who scored during the 1957 season.

Not much is remembered or written about the entire 4th quarter, other than this: the Blythe Black Panthers were a class act. They did *not* give up and held Cass scoreless in the last 12 minutes of the game.

Now Cass had three games left to play in the regular season.

"Only three games stand between Cass Township and the greatest season in the school's history."
The Pottsville Republican, Oct 22, 1957

Chapter 13

Fifth Home Game in a Row

Game 7 (7-0) at Home vs. Mahanoy Township
Monday, Oct 28, 1957

Another Monday night game and Cass' last home game, unbelievably their fifth in a row, unheard of in today's balanced scheduling. You might expect this would be another high scoring affair, because Cass had not travelled since September 21st, over a month prior. They had the home field advantage with great local fan support - again. But this was a tough and determined Mahanoy Township team that Cass was facing. Yet again, another team which wanted to be the *first* to score against Cass and to knock them off the undefeated category. Coach Bill Buck Jones had prepared his "Purple Larks" so very well that this game was almost the end of the perfect season. Except for one thing - an unlikely hero. Of course, none of the guys on the Cass team would ever use the term "hero" as they were team players through and through.

Coach Pat would later be quoted as saying this 1957 team as well the following Cass 1958 team were "...the most unselfish, humble, and caring bunch of guys I was ever associated with in about a half century of playing and coaching. It is astonishing how they put the team first. No individual records, no statistics impressed them, except winning."

Eerily, similar to the second game of the season at Nescopeck and the fifth game at home against Ashland, the Cass Condors did not score during the first quarter. They led only 7-0 at halftime, the third time of the season.

Cass won the coin toss, and instead of electing to start on defense (their usual strategy), received the opening kickoff. They started off with gusto and efficiently drove down the field, with some great blocks up front and fine running by all the backs:

Beakley Ryan, Tony Antonelli, and Harry Heffron. They stalled only 28 yards from the goal line, when Cass tried to catch the Larks sleeping. They faked handoffs and threw two incomplete passes. Play went up and down the field until Cass ended up on 4th down with their backs at their own 1-yd line, very dangerous territory indeed. But no worries: Dave Gauntlett made the perfect snap, and the line blocked strong and hard, while Gus punted Cass out of harm's way.

The Larks took possession and made a series of good plays driving Cass all the way back to their own 10-yd line. The notorious "bend but don't break" defense then shut down the Larks, when their quarterback Lee Houser overthrew his receiver in the Cass end zone. This was one of the scariest moments of the UNSCORED UPON season.

Now that Cass had escaped the Larks scoring threat, they had 90 yards ahead of them. The Condors began *the* drive of the ballgame, making first downs and covering about 70 yards of real estate in 12 plays. An important play was one of only two completed passes in the game for Cass: Russ Frantz caught a jump pass inside the 20-yd line.

Two plays later, it looked like another run, but it was a fake. Beakley took the direct snap and handed the ball to quarterback Wash Brennan. Brennan thought he could sneak another pass to Russ Frantz or Harry Butsko, but was pressured by Mahanoy Township's defense, so he went into scramble mode. In this, only his second varsity start of the season, what would sophomore Wash do? Would he find an open receiver or toss the ball up for grabs on this third down play? Neither, since he was small but very quick. He sprinted to the right behind some great blocking and ran 16 yards all the way into the end zone. Cass was now ahead 6-0. No kicking extra points lately, so halfback Tony Antonelli took the ball over the middle to make it 7-0 going into the halftime break.

The second half was a stalemate, with mistakes and fumbles on both sides of the ball. The second half was not a thing of beauty. Every time Cass was unable to make first downs, they used secret weapon Gus Gressik to punt them out of trouble. Once in the 4th and final quarter, Gus boomed the ball all the way inside the Larks 30 yard line, where the Condors held the Larks until they were forced to punt on 4th down. With Beakley Ryan back to receive the punt, anything could happen. The little guy did not disappoint. Ryan caught the punt on his own 30-yd line and ran it back over 55 yards. With only a few minutes left in the game, could Cass easily put this one out of reach with a score? It was not to be. After making one first down, Cass only made it as far as the Mahanoy Township Purple Larks 25-yd line, where the Larks took over.

After Mahanoy Township's first three plays, which lost four yards, the Larks' Coach Jones sent in a play to go for it on 4th down, from his own 20-yd line. This was a gutsy call, but behind 7-0 and with time running out, he really had nothing to lose. Cass held and took over with about a minute to go. Coach Pat played it smart and safe, as he did not want to blow a sure win just for an "easy score." After two running plays, time ran out, with Cass on the 10-yd line. But a win is a win, and Cass had done it again.

This was a Monday night football game to remember since Cass not only won this game by a score of 7-0, but now had an undefeated 7 wins and 0 losses all season with only two regular season games to go. (7-0 in the game and 7-0 on the season, get it?) Lucky sevens! This game, though a victory, presented some foreshadowing: Mahanoy Township would end Cass Township's 15-game UNSCORED UPON streak. The following year (1958) in the 5th game, Mahanoy Township beat Cass 6-0. Another hard fought battle, Mahanoy Township would be the only team to score against Cass in two entire football seasons!

Chapter 14

Only Four Days Later

Game 8 (14-0) at Lansford
Friday, Nov 1, 1957

After five straight home game shutouts, Cass had to play the last two games on the road. This was tough and thanks to the postponed game back on October 17th, Cass had been forced into a sequence of two straight Monday night games. Now they had a Friday night game, just four days later! Imagine that in today's high school environment of safety and rules! Not likely.

To their disadvantage, that left only three days to practice: Tuesday, Wednesday, and Thursday after school. They had to travel to play the Lansford "Panthers" on a Friday night. The Panthers had a good ball club, and had only lost one game so far (to Tamaqua, PA) that season. What could be worse? Answer: the weather! It was not just inclement - that Friday evening it rained and poured right up to game time. Though the Cass team was ready, they were not exactly well-rested. These days, hard rain typically postpones high school football games. But unless it was a hurricane, in the 1950s the game was on. Both teams' officials met in the rain prior to the game and agreed to play, despite the elements imploring them to call it off. Someone even brought up the flu season, and thought it dangerous to play under those nasty weather conditions. If there was any good news, it was that Cass had worked in a few really tough practices. They were able to re-focus, and Coach Pat told the team to "look forward to Friday, not backwards at Monday," and to play solid defense.

Here is where it gets both interesting and frustrating. With the rain, would this be the fourth game of the perfect season where the mighty Cass Condors went into the halftime locker room leading only 7-0? Yep, another low scoring game was in the making. This was a defensive match right up there with their best performances, as Cass did not allow the Panthers even one first down in the entire first half. Sportswriter Ronnie Christ even gave "ink" to Steve Kachmar, Joe Hydock, and Russ Frantz for their solid defensive play, which kept the ball in play on the Panthers side of the soggy football field. Of course, Gus Gressik gets credit here with his excellent punting, booting the ball deep whenever Cass was unable to move the ball. This ensured that when Lansford got the ball, they started deep in their own territory. Needless to say, without the fine single wing hikes from center Dave Gauntlett, Cass could easily have fumbled an off-target snap on this wet and rain-soaked field. Again, Cass displayed a total team effort through and through.

The rain guaranteed that a ground game would be played. Cass only completed one pass, Lansford none. The game started with a promising kickoff return by Brennan when he returned it all the way past mid-field. But the offense sputtered and Gus punted it away after three plays, so now the Panthers were stuck deep at their own 28-yd line. After two fumbles, which they recovered themselves, Lansford had to punt, and that was all the momentum Cass needed. Beakley, the usual Cass return man caught the wet punt at mid-field and ran it back into Panther territory. Cass now ran the ball for a dozen plays, eating up the clock in most of the first quarter, and set it up on the one yard line with a first down. Weiner Antonelli got his jersey number called, and dove in for the touchdown, bowling his way over several Panthers. He did such a good job that the guys gave him the ball again on the extra point try, and he easily ran it in.

Tony Phillips, during a time out, asked Coach Pat what he could do about a Lansford player throwing muddy sand in his face and wondered, "Why can't the official throw a flag?" He remembered Coach Pat telling him, "Just hit him harder - he'll stop." The second quarter was sloppy, and the key plays featured a few fumbles by the Panthers, one of which Gus Gressik recovered for Cass on the Panthers 25-yd line. This was surely great field position for Cass to take advantage of and work the ball into the end zone. But that did not happen. Cass could only move the Panthers about five yards and gave up the ball on downs. The half ended with Cass ahead only 7-0.

Not a whole lot is known or remembered about what was said during that tense halftime. One would think Cass would have this routine down to a science after the fourth time that season with this exact half time score, 7-0. The only adjustments the players remember discussing were to continue the pressure on the Panthers defensively and to continue to keep pounding the ball by running strong. They were to keep the ball on the ground during the remaining 24 minutes of the game - the second half. Coach Pat was known for this philosophy on passing: "When you put the ball in the air, there are only three things that can happen, and two of them are bad" (incomplete and interception).

After a kickoff to the Panthers, the ball rolled out of bounds. The Panthers started on their own 40-yd line, by rule. Cass' game plan was working well, and they totally shut down the Panthers, who had to punt on 4th down. The Panthers' punter, Bob Early, barely got the punt off, after about three Cass defenders almost blocked his kick. The ball only made it a few yards, not quite to midfield. The Condors offense now had another golden opportunity to maintain the momentum and work the ball all the way to the goal line. But after only two running plays, Beakley took the direct snap and ran around the right end, defying gravity yet again, and staying on his feet. He executed some amazing cuts on the rain-soaked field, behind a few good blocks. He did the rest himself. He ran back across the field, and sprinted 41 yards to score without a Lansford Panther even touching him. Antonelli pounded it in for the extra point and Cass had the lead that would hold up, 14-0.

Some remaining game highlights include Cass holding the Panthers to only one first down and only 42 yards of total offense. On a punt in the third quarter, the Panthers' punter, Early, was pressured again. This time Russ Frantz blasted over his guy and solidly blocked the punt. Joe Hydock recovered and ran the ball all the way to the 17-yd line. (Remember this play when I describe the end of the Shamokin playoff game in Chapter 17, Playoff Game in the Mud. You will see the irony.)

Could Cass easily score and make it three touchdowns to ice the game against the Panthers? Not on this rainy, muddy field: Lansford did not give up. They showed toughness and held Cass for four plays, after Cass had a first down and goal to go at the Panthers 7-yd line. The rest of the fourth quarter was a seesaw event where defenses prevailed, and the offenses could not make first downs. Cass felt a slight amount of relief: most of the action was contained to the Panthers side of the 50-yd line.

Cass' season record was now 8-0, "undefeated, untied, and unscored upon" and most importantly, in first place in the Southern Division of the PA Eastern State Conference. Unknown to anyone but the football gods, this game was an eerily similar dress rehearsal for playing in horrible field conditions. They would have to play in the rain and mud at the end of the season in a playoff game at Pottsville, PA.

The buzz in Schuylkill County offices, stores, bars, pool halls, diners, mills, mines, and *The Pottsville Republican* newspaper was that Cass was an unbelievable high school football team, but certainly due for a loss, or at least a score against them in their last scheduled game of the season, next Saturday against St. Clair.

(Frank Machita in picture)

Chapter 15

Saturday Afternoon Football

Game 9 (13-0) at St. Clair
Saturday, Nov 9, 1957

Good news, bad news. The good news: unlike the prior week, Cass had seven days to recover, and worked in five good practice sessions. The bad news: they had to play another away game, and

against the strong and high scoring St. Clair ball club.

The build up from the press and fans was extraordinary. Why? This annual rivalry was the last regularly scheduled game of the season. Cass was on a winning streak never before experienced in Schuylkill County sports: they held all opponents "scoreless," or a new term that was now being used more frequently - **UNSCORED UPON**. They could establish new school and county records as the greatest defensive high school team ever by winning the big Saturday game against St. Clair.

On the much read Friday night edition of *The Pottsville Republican*, the top sports story featured, as you might have figured, the Cass-St Clair game predictions: this included statistics and even a photo showing seven of Cass' defenders standing near their goal line, with hands extended as if to say "Stay out" or "Get back!" The paper superimposed a photo of St. Clair's Coach, Bill Wolff glaring down at the players, pondering how to score on these guys. Coach Wolff's Saints had only lost two games all year, and scored in *all* their games. They fully expected to at least score, and if not upset Cass, at least play the role of "spoiler." After all, the Saints scored 187 points so far to their opponents' 95 points.

For those adding up Cass' points in the first eight games, it tallied 208. There was even a strong revenge motive for the Saints: the previous 1956 season, the Saints were undefeated. They had shut out Cass by a score of 25-0 in the final game. The now seniors (who were juniors on the 1956 teams) certainly remembered playing each other the prior year as if it were yesterday, except now the situation was reversed and *Cass* was the undefeated team.

Coach Wolff humbly and respectfully predicted a tough battle. He was quoted in the paper stating "Squad spirit is high, and every boy on our squad is shooting for an upset." He went on, "I feel certain we will put on a good show." Coach Pat on the other hand was a bit more willing to go out on a limb and was quoted as saying, "I am completely confident we can finish the season with a perfect record. I don't think we are overconfident." In a display of respect for the Saints team and his friend Coach Wolff, he said, "Stopping the St. Clair offense may be our toughest assignment of the season."

The tension mounted. Only one score in the first half, but Cass dominated the running game. Cass played most of the first 24 minutes where they loved to be - on the Saints' side of the 50-yd line. One of Gus Gressik's best punts of the year went out of bounds at about the Saints' 3-yd line.

After holding St. Clair deep in their territory, Cass ended the 12-minute first period with the ball on the Saint's 18-yd line. The score was 0-0. The second period started with an exciting run by

Frank Machita, where Frank almost scored, but was finally brought down inside the 5-yd line. On the second play of the second quarter, Beakley Ryan got his chance and made a classic "Beakley" tough four yard leaning-forward style run on the strong side of the unbalanced Cass line. He scored the touchdown behind the block of right tackle Tony Phillips. The Saints stopped a hard charging Tony Antonelli on the extra point run, and the score remained 6-0, which is what it was remained going into halftime.

During the rest of the second period, both teams played tough football but were unable to score again. Coach Wolff must have decided Cass defense was too tough to run against, so he started his usually successful passing attack. But St. Clair only completed 2 of 13 passes the entire game, both in the second half.

So imagine the feeling as Cass goes into the visiting team locker room only leading by a single score. Tension? Maybe by now, you would think they were used to this feeling, as they had already experienced low scoring first halves in four games that season, most recently the prior week against Lansford. Now they had to clear their heads and just focus on the remaining 24 minutes of the regular season, nothing else. Coach Pat told the guys to stay focused and give it all they had. He asked them to reach down and play the best football of their lives. "This one is for all of you," he said. "Play your guts out."

But remember, these were 16 and 17 year old boys. They still chuckled about the one play where Charlie Zurat, on defense, jumped over the Saints' offensive line, long before the center snapped the ball, and whistles blew and flags were thrown. Over

50 years later, they still remembered this play when we spoke about that game.

In the home locker room, Coach Wolff must have been proud indeed. The score was only 6-0 and could have been a lot worse. He was a good coach and a gentleman and stressed the positive to his "squad," as he called them, and told them to not give up. The Saints all knew they were only one play away from tying this game (and maybe going ahead with the extra point) and Bill Wolff tried to fire them up for the upset of the season. He surely implied that to beat the local Cass rival was a game they would never forget.

This was it. With less than one-half hour of football, some of the seniors who had no college aspirations, had to realize this likely would be the last time they would play football in their young lives (they could not realize there would be a playoff game). Both teams were excited, but for different reasons: one team wanted to finish the regular season perfectly, the other wanted to play the spoiler role! To add to the suspense, no one scored during the third quarter, but the Saints made it exciting. Senior quarterback Mike Botto threw a nice pass to young sophomore St. Clair end, Bill Holley, who ran for over 30 yards before being brought down from behind by Harry Heffron (they became friends later in life as adults). The Saints continued the drive all the way to the Condors' 13-yd line, where Cass dug in and held. After a defensive struggle the rest of the third period, Cass held the Saints deep in their territory again. Beakley Ryan, who scored earlier, now saw Saints quarterback Botto dare to try to throw a ball in his area. He intercepted it right near the Saints' own 20-yd line.

Going into the final 12 minutes, Cass had a great chance to score and crush the hopes of St. Clair's fans and players. On the very second play, Wash Brennan connected with a 20 yard pass to left end Harry Butsko. He did not break his stride and made it all the way into the end zone for the touchdown. With Frank Machita not attempting extra points since October 10th, almost a month earlier, there would be no kicking. Machita crashed in for the extra point. The score was now Cass 13, St Clair 0.

But there was still time on the clock, and Cass had to remain poised to finish the game and the regular season UNSCORED upon. They could not let their guard down. With the adrenaline high, Coach Bill Wolff on the St. Clair sideline was not about to give up. He wanted to score quickly and still win the game, so he decided it was time to reach into his bag of trick plays. He called for Botto to hand off to halfback, Jack Prokop, who then would drop back to pass. He did exactly that, and in the confusion, quarterback Botto sneaked into the clear. Prokop found him open and heaved it downfield.

The 6 ft 1 inch Botto caught the ball and looked like he was going to make it all the way to the end zone for the score. In those few seconds, hearts sank on the Cass side of the field: there was the touchdown they did not think would happen - and it didn't! After the longest play of the game, 50 yards, the slow-footed Mike Botto was brought down from behind at the Cass 20-yd line by Cass' all-purpose player, Frank Machita. (The Cass players kiddingly called Botto "Lead-foot.") That was the last chance for St. Clair. The rest of the game was uneventful except for what must have been hearts beating fast, sweat dripping, and eyes looking up at the clock as it ticked toward 00:00 remaining.

Cass had done it! They had remained focused and scored 221 points during the season, and the combined score of all their opponents remained at zero. No thoughts of glory and no gloating. They were just one happy bunch of teen-aged buddies and teammates who had done the impossible, together. The season may have been short, but the record and the memories would last a lifetime. All that remained was to be patient and wait for the playoffs. And they would practice and practice on their Cass home football field in the coming weeks.

At this point in time, Cass was way ahead of Shamokin in the standings. It was not even close. Cass thought they were just waiting to see whom they had to play in the Northern Division to be Pennsylvania's Eastern Conference champion. Or so they thought. Some teams only played four or five games all season due to the killer flu. The Shamokin Greyhounds had to win an incredible four games within a 13 day period to creep ahead of Cass by Thanksgiving Day. Now comes some statistical wizardry. Shamokin ended up .002 ahead of Cass.

In the picture below, I was at the Saturday St. Clair game. That is me in the picture with my dad, between Steve Yuschock (#12) and Steve Kachmar (#17).

Chapter 16

Championship Controversy

The controversy all began when the Shamokin Greyhounds played against the Mt Carmel Red Tornadoes on their much hyped Thanksgiving Day annual extravaganza. This was an amazing Pennsylvania coal region local headline here from *The Shamokin News-Dispatch,* Greyhounds Win 12-0.

Shamokin Stands Jammed for Big Game

The photograph above shows the crowded Shamokin stands during the school's annual Turkey Day classic against Mount Carmel yesterday in Kemp Memorial Stadium. The paid attendance was listed at 5,867. (News-Dispatch Photo).

The rivalry went back all the way to 1908. The teams faithfully played each other most every year. through WWI, WWII, and the Korean War. Mt. Carmel led the series with 28 wins to only 10 wins for Shamokin. They tied 10 times. That is a lot of years and ballgames - 48! So it is no wonder that this annual rivalry game was a big deal. And it was well-attended! Over **5,800 fans** watched this home game for the mighty Greyhounds.

Four High Schools Cop Football Titles In Holiday Games

By BURTON W. SIGLIN
United Press Sports Writer

Newly-won titles today graced the trophy rooms of Lancaster, Carlisle, Scranton Central and Shamokin on the strength of climactic victories in Thanksgiving Day football contests.

From a Cass point of view, if Mt. Carmel would have beat Shamokin, there would be no controversy. Cass would have been the immediate champs of the Southern Division. But it was not to be. Mt. Carmel was a strong football team, coached by veteran coach, Mike Terry, with a record of 8-2. And the Shamokin Greyhounds, coached by a young second year coach, Lou Sorrentino, had already played 11 football games. They came in with an even better record with one more win, at 9-2. And what a defensive battle it was! Mt Carmel scored in every

"If you don't read the newspaper, you are uninformed. If you do read the newspaper, you are misinformed." Mark Twain

game that season coming into the Thanksgiving thriller. So with a halftime score of 0-0, they had to be a bit worried. Little did Coach Terry realize his team would not even get a first down in the second half!

No one scored until the fourth quarter when two of their great backs, Laughlin and Schickley, both scored on great runs. That is when the Shamokin team came alive in that rainy game. When The Greyhounds won the game by a score of 12-0, they believed that they had just won the Pennsylvania Interscholastic Athletic Association (PIAA) Southern Division Championship of the PA Eastern Conference. Their record was now 10-2, the best Shamokin High school record since 1940! And similar to Cass, Shamokin was unscored upon for six of their ten victories. Shamokin was no doubt a great defensive ball club. Of course the Cass faithful, who had rooted for a Mt Carmel victory, were clearly disappointed.

Note the excerpt from the Nov 29, 1957 edition of *The Shamokin News-Dispatch*. It seems to be the very first publication to include an article by the United Press stating "Shamokin Greyhounds climaxed an uphill drive by rapping Mt Carmel 12-0, to edge undefeated and untied Cass Township for the Southern Division title." Not so fast Mr. Siglin! In fairness to the UPI writer, he states that the championships are still unofficial. But one thing was for sure: Scranton Central beat Scranton Tech badly in the Northern Division, 40-7, so Scranton Central would clearly be the Northern Division Champ.

On the day after the game, the Friday after Thanksgiving, there is an article in *The Shamokin News Dispatch* stating they will play against Scranton Central on Dec 7, 1957, at home at Kemp Memorial Stadium, Edgewood Park if unofficial standings hold up.

> *And now, if unofficial standings hold up, the Greyhounds will play one of the school's most important games in history December 7 against Scranton Central in Kemp Stadium.*

They would not! The Shamokin faithful believed they had won the Southern Division, and even knew who they would play, the date and the place. Scranton Central believed they would have to play one more game. They would not!

Even the great *Pottsville Republican* sportswriter Walter Farquhar wrote something about Cass that proved to be wrong. In the Friday edition, he wrote, "Scranton Central and Old Forge are the Northern Division's main contenders, with the winner to meet Shamokin in Southern Division area this season." Walter was seldom proven wrong.

SHAMOKIN NEWS-DISPATCH, SHAMOKIN, PA., FRIDAY, NOVEMBER 20, 1937   PAGE ELEVEN

Cass Protests Shamokin's Claim to Title

Unknown to Scranton and Shamokin, action was simultaneously going on at Cass headquarters (Coach Pat's home). Late in the evening on Thanksgiving Day, after Scranton beat Mt. Carmel, my dad just had to be burning up the phone line. His Cass team had a better record at 9-0, as they were undefeated and unscored upon. Dad would not take a statistical defeat without a fight!

Region School Charges 2 Foes Were Denied Right to Play Postponed Contests

Complaint to Be Filed With Conference During Meeting Tomorrow in Hazleton

Shamokin High unofficially captured the Southern Division title in the Eastern Football Conference by blanking Mount Carmel, 12-0, in yesterday's Turkey Day classic,

In their Friday edition, (headline above) *The Shamokin News-Dispatch* reported, "A spokesman for Cass Township revealed last night his school (Cass) will present the complaint before a meeting of the Eastern Conference tomorrow in Hazelton. Unofficial standings in the Southern Division show Shamokin finished in front with a mark of .594 points, while Cass wound up a step behind with .592." A step? The figure .002 is not a step, it is more like a blink of an eye.

The report continues, "Cass defeated Lansford and West Mahanoy Township during the regular season. Should either contest be played, of which there is little likelihood, and should either Lansford or West Mahanoy win, Cass would receive sufficient points to move ahead of Shamokin in final conference standings." Fair and balanced!

Interestingly, *The Shamokin News-Dispatch* continues, "If conference officials abide by rules and regulations of their organization, and there is no reason to believe they will not, Cass' complaint cannot cause Shamokin any trouble." I guess in that sentence they were playing to their hometown audience.

This is where the whole issue of who was in first place became very complicated and thick with math and statistics. The official league statistician was a man named Fred Dawson. He must have been an amazing mathematician, and one cannot imagine the pressure he must have been under. There were no computers available, no Excel spreadsheets, only hand held calculators. And back then, most folks did not even own one of those calculators. They were too expensive!

Shamokin to Take Legal Action If Cass Wins Southern Title

As you see, it boiled down to Shamokin with a reported two thousandth of a point lead in the complex computations .594 to .592. Talk about numerical intricacy!

Pat was so angry about the implication of these statistics, he quoted the old expression, "Figures don't lie, but liars figure." He was a chemistry and science teacher, not a math wizard. He was, however, smarter than the average bear, and could hold his own in math, as well as the next guy. But, really? .002?

As fate would have it, Pat did have a secret weapon of his own, an unknown factor which would boost his case. His loyal former player, Alvin "Al" Beretsky, starting Cass basketball player from the prior year, 1956, knew something he had to share with Pat. Al still lived in the area, and had been to every Cass football game.

This has never been publicly revealed, so here goes. Al was talking to his Uncle, Metro "Menna" Warischalk about Cass statistics. Menna did not get how Cass could *possibly* be behind Shamokin. You see, Menna was a former coal miner and had been paralyzed from the waist down in a horrible mining accident a decade earlier. He was always a smart man, but since the accident, he became an avid sports fan and kept statistics on everything sports related, especially his team, Cass Township. He understood some of the complex calculations the Eastern Conference officials used about weighted averages in "strength of schedule", opponents' win-loss records, conference games, etc.

Remember, this was a deadly flu season and some of the teams only played a few games that year. So, through no fault of the Cass' team, some of the opponents they beat did not play enough games to give Cass the extra conference points they needed to move ahead statistically. Menna weighted some factors differently and proved to Al that Cass could actually be ahead of Shamokin. Al remembers Uncle Menna's exact words, "Cass was screwed" in this complex rating system. The conference rating system gave any winning team points when a defeated opponent won other games. Menna said it was a "snow job." You see, he was a statistical genius, but still a down to earth man of few words.

When Al realized that Pat might need a helping hand, he contacted his close friends, football players Weiner Antonelli and Russ Frantz. He explained that Menna had back-up figures, and convinced his friends that they had important information to help Coach Pat and the team. The three jumped into Al's trusty old 1950 Buick and drove the two miles down the hill to Minersville. They knocked on Pat's door. (Many folks were too poor to have a phone in those days.)

In fairness to my dad, he would have still strongly argued Cass' case - stats or no stats! All who knew him state that he was a fiery, emotional, loyal, and competitive man. He was! He had no intention of letting his team come this far and not get a fair chance to compete on the field of play for the championship. He felt he owed it to the team and to Cass fans. As a young child, I was a sports fan. I can still clearly remember my dad saying, "How can a team that is 8-1 be ahead of us at 8-0?" (He was referring to eight wins in conference games.) So, Pat immediately contacted league officials again, but this time he stated he now had figures to back up his facts. To say this issue was bitterly contested would be an understatement! Coach Pat Droskinis was about to enter into the toughest fight of his coaching career, and it would not be on the playing field!

There was a chance that Cass could advance to the Eastern Conference Championship game against Scranton Central if two teams agreed to play a postponed game against each other, Lansford and Summit Hill. If Lansford won that game, it would give Cass sufficient statistical points to move ahead of Shamokin. Remember that Cass had beaten Lansford, a conference team, back on November 1, 1957. But the league could not force Lansford and Summit Hill to play against each other, so the school officials had to agree to play. The problem was that Summit Hill had absolutely no reason to play that football game. They were 0-3 in league play and stated that all their football equipment was cleaned and in storage 'til next year. They had played their last game three weeks prior, on November 9th. Conference officials gave them a Monday night deadline, December 2nd, to decide if they would play the make-up game.

Another detail lost in most sports history is that Lansford would have gladly agreed to play another football game. The team was fresh and had just played on Thanksgiving Day. They lost that game to Coaldale. If Lansford had beaten Coaldale, Cass would have moved past Shamokin in statistical points and would have been declared the Southern Conference champion, hands down. There would have been no disagreement, no argument, no need to discuss anything. Shamokin knew this. See? I warned you it was complicated! But Lansford lost, so Shamokin now had a case to make.

But Shamokin had absolutely no sympathy for team officials not willing to play make up games. The Shamokin Greyhounds had just played on Thanksgiving Day and beat Mt Carmel 12-0. Including that victory, they had just valiantly played four games in a 13-day period to stay in contention with Cass. *The Shamokin News-Dispatch* referred to this as, "an unprecedented ordeal in scholastic football ranks." No doubt it was! If not for this feat, Cass would have been ahead in the standings. Way ahead.

Saturday, November 30, 1957

The league met on Saturday night, in Hazleton, PA. Both *The Pottsville Republican* and *The Shamokin News-Dispatch* referred to the meeting as a "stormy four-hour session." The conference had 53 members, and this was such a high profile, important issue that 48 members showed up on that Thanksgiving holiday weekend. It was also referred to as a "bedlam of confusion," "contentious," and a "dispute-studded get together," just to name a few of the milder descriptions. A fired up Coach Pat Droskinis led the Cass delegation and was the unofficial chief litigator, according to sources. Years later, I was told that my dad earned his honorary law degree that Saturday night. He was only 42 years old.

The Shamokin delegation was led by Shamokin's Principal Paul Swank. Mr. Swank vehemently argued that even if Lansford played Summit Hill, it still would not be enough to declare Cass the winner. He pointed out a conference rule that required teams to play a minimum of five conference games. And Summit Hill was seemingly not going to play two more games! The controversial battle continued. It boiled down to the representatives from Northumberland County supporting Shamokin and the ones from Schuylkill County supporting Cass Township. Jim Boran, Minersville's athletic director, was involved in most discussions, since he was the head of the arbitration board. Coach Pat and Mr. Boran knew each other: they had worked together in Minersville High School. They were friends, but Jim Boran was a fair and honest man and could be professional and objective.

The Pottsville Republican interviewed Coach Droskinis (They usually accidentally misspelled his name "Droskin**as**"). Here is their report: "Cass Township Coach Pat Droskinas reported that the stormy session at Hazleton Saturday lasted approximately five hours.

"The first issue brought up stated that Cass Township and Shamokin should play for the Southern Division title. This motion was defeated by a vote of the conference schools. Coach Droskinas first argued against the move, but later said he would gladly play Shamokin to decide the championship. Shamokin was against the move.

"Droskinas took the floor and issued his protests on the grounds that a Lansford victory over Summit Hill would give his team the title. He took issue with the conference for waiting too long to start any action on the postponed games.

"It was one long argument," said Droskinas. "At one point I

had the floor for over thirty minutes trying to make my position clear. Every move made was voted down by the Northern Division teams."

Monday December 2, 1957

Conference president Frank Thornton stated they had "requested" Summit Hill school officials to complete the conference scheduled games with Lansford and McAdoo. The teams could not be forced to play and they did not. Summit Hill had no real reason to play Lansford. If they had played against Lansford, they would then have to play one additional game. It would be against McAdoo, to satisfy the five conference game requirement. That would have caused chaos in both the Northern and Southern Divisions, as a final North-South playoff game would have been delayed until late December. That was a non-starter.

The Shamokin News-Dispatch reported fully on the details of the stormy Saturday night league meeting in Hazleton. Part of that report states, " ... but Shamokin may have emerged the winner if several conferees, who grew weary over riotous haranguing, had not left the room." Colorful phrasing!

Tuesday Dec 3, 1957

Eastern Conference Calls Special Meeting For Tonight; Funk Frowns on Extensions

Now, strangely, there was a report that Summit Hill indeed wanted to play the two postponed football games. PIAA Executive Director Mark Funk was in a pickle. According to *The Shamokin News-Dispatch*, "Conference officials always have required member schools to close their seasons at Thanksgiving with the conference championship game played 10 days later. Funk pointed out that PIAA regulations demand that teams have a full three weeks of practice. He said this rule is enforced for the protection of the boys – the time spread permits them to get in shape for the season." He continued, "You can realize the dim view the PIAA takes of these games when this team has not played or practiced in a month."

So one can only imagine the catch 22 dilemma the PIAA found itself in. If all these games were played in the Southern Division of the Eastern Football Conference, it would seriously delay the playoff game between the final winner, and the already declared Northern Division champion, Scranton Central. And when would that be - after Christmas?

This was such a serious sports matter that The Eastern PA Scholastic Football Conference called a special meeting Tuesday evening near Hazelton, PA. *The Shamokin News-Dispatch* reported that conference president, Frank Thornton, said the purpose was "to discuss further the status of the conference in regards to the playoff for the conference title." They made an immediate request for all hands on deck and that representatives from all conference schools attend the special meeting. The last sentence of the article implied the finality of that meeting, "Definite word is expected to be given during the session as to the naming of a Southern Division championship team." Not exactly!

Wednesday, December 4, 1957

The compromise decision ... **FINALLY**:

Shamokin and Cass to Clash Saturday for Right to Claim Southern Division Honors

Exact story from the *front page* (not the sports page) of the 20-page edition of *The Shamokin News-Dispatch:*

"The bitterly contested decision over who should be champion of the Southern Division of the Eastern Football Conference for

1957 was amicably resolved last night when Shamokin and Cass Township backed by unanimous approval of the 53 school circuit, agreed to battle each other for the disputed honor."

"In a move climaxing one of the most heated verbal struggles in state schoolboy athletic annals, which went as far as threatened legal action, Shamokin yielded to a numerically superior Schuylkill County coalition and volunteered to take on the unscored upon Cass eleven.

"The contest, regarded as a "natural," because of the outstanding records of each school, will be staged Saturday afternoon in Pottsville stadium. Time for the kickoff has been set for 1:30 PM.

"Fighting relentlessly, but vainly to have their amazing Greyhounds crowned as divisional champs, on the strength of a .588 to .569 (the statistics had been recalculated) lead in percentage points, Shamokin delegates to the conference meeting at Hazelton capitulated to repeated setbacks in parliamentary procedure.

"Headed by Principal Paul A. Swank, who served as spokesman throughout the wearisome ordeal, Shamokin decided: since sentiment appears to favor Cass Township, Shamokin moves that Shamokin and Cass Township play for the Southern Division Championship.

"While the city school resorted to what many least expected, Shamokin was warmly lauded."

The article went on to then report that the motion was "for the best interests of the conference."

"The overwhelming voting strength of Shamokin's adversaries in the conference sessions became evident in climaxing moments of last night's three-hour meeting. The gathering, in which 29 of the conference's members participated, to represent a quorum, was for the most part harmonious and cooperative in contrast to last Saturday's drawn out melee of harangues and disorder."

Later in the article it states, "Shamokin's defeat permeated the atmosphere in a parade of speeches favoring the stand of Cass Township. Spokesmen from Summit Hill, McAdoo, Lansford, Swoyersville and others implicitly supported Cass' right to the championship claim. Shamokin received no backing from the floor on the long debated question of the motion."

"Cass Township, whose chief spokesman was Coach Pat Droskinas (sic), appeared to capture sufficient sentiment of the conferees by protesting Swank's motion on grounds that rescinding of Saturday's action would make Shamokin the division champ."

Finally the article addresses the post-game situation, since Scranton Central awaited the results in the Northern Division. "There is a possibility that the Southern Division champ will not play Scranton Central at all. Scranton said it will not play the title contest on any day other than December 7. Shamokin, should it defeat Cass for the division banner, is similarly committed to play no football after Saturday."

For the record, Coach Pat Droskinis, backed by School Board President Jimmy Ryan, said Cass Township would play Scranton Central "anytime, anywhere, and anyplace."

In an almost prophetic motion, "The conference approved a motion by Coal Township stipulating that if the game ends in a tie, a toss of a coin would decide the Southern Division Champ." And the game almost did just that!

Now Cass had just two days to make final preparations. They had not played since Saturday, November 9th. It was now Dec. 4th. Shamokin was no doubt more game-ready. They had just played the previous week on Thanksgiving Day. Both teams won their previous games by shutouts, almost identical scores! Cass won 13-0 and Shamokin won by a score of 12-0.

Cass had not played a football game for almost a month, but they had been practicing for the past three weeks. And they were practicing against tough opponents, each other! They had already played all nine of their regular season games, and now had to assume they may be playing the Northern Division champs. But according to the players I interviewed, they did not care who they played, they just wanted to work out and be ready to win.

Just like regular season practices, they either worked out on their rocky practice field, located at the South Cass Fire Company, or occasionally, they just used their regular field adjacent to the school. When it rained really hard, they still had to practice, but Coach Pat used the gym. Cass had decided to delay the start of their basketball season, since some of the same players were still practicing football. This included starters, Wash Brennan, Dave Gauntlett, Gus Gressik, Weiner Antonelli, Harry Butsko, and Russ Frantz.

The unsung heroes, mentioned in the chapter called "Secret Weapons," did it again. The varsity and jayvee players who were backups practiced hard against the starting lineup. They hit hard, took the blocks, and kept their starters sharp and in shape. Besides, they also had to be in shape and know all the offensive and defensive plays, since they were only a play away from being called into action. An illness or serious injury could knock a starter out of any game. The starters knew that, as they already lost their senior quarterback, Ted Wannisky. That was the day Brennan got promoted from jayvee quarterback to starting quarterback. Early in the season, they lost another potential starter, George "Whitey" Sinko, who broke his leg in practice.

Decades later, Coach Pat and the starters still credited their second string players for helping Cass perform at the level it did. Guys like Ron Ney, Rich Krasnitsky, Mike Milyo, and Joe Witcofsky went the extra mile for the team. (The jayvee players helped too. They are listed in the appendix.)

Coach Pat stated many times that the entire team comprised a group of the most unselfish and dedicated athletes he ever played sports with or coached. And Coach Pat played a lot of sports and coached a lot of teams.

After the decision for Cass and Shamokin to play for the championship, Cass' athletes had only two days to prepare for the playoff game. Finally!

Cass Twp. Rolls Up Biggest Margin In Series With Battling Miners, 27-0

Cass Routs Nescopeck

Cass Routs W. Mahanoy

Haven Cass Victim.

Cass Nips Ashland

Cass Clubs Blythe

Cass Nips Mahanoy Twp.

Cass Hands Lansford Setback

Cass Twp. Beats St. Clair

Ball Rolls Out of End Zone As Cass Nips Shamokin, 2-0

Chapter 17

Playoff Game in the Mud

Game 10 (2-0) Pottsville Veterans Stadium vs. Shamokin
Saturday, Dec 7, 1957

Shamokin and Cass Battle Today for Division Crown

After almost a month off, and the stress of not knowing if they'd get the chance to play again, the big game was finally at hand. Remember, this was the same Cass team that played earlier in the season with only four days between games. Now they had been off for four weeks except for practice. Would they be rusty? Complacent? Or maybe feel a bit overconfident? Or would they be the cool and confident team that Coach Pat hoped and prayed they would be? On the other side of the field, the Shamokin Greyhounds must have been a bit beaten up and tired. Amazingly, this would be their fifth game in a 22 day period!

Thousands of Pennsylvanians listened to this game on Pottsville's WPPA live radio broadcast, and I was one of them despite being only five years old. There is also grainy game footage available on YouTube (look up "Cass football" "Shamokin playoff game"). Every play was filmed on 16mm film that was worn out long before it could become the digitized version available there. Using his trusty old reel-to-reel projector, Coach Pat featured this playoff game footage at many banquets and gatherings in the decades of the 70s, 80s and 90s. Since I was too young to remember anything but the final play, this chapter is based on a play-by-play review of the game footage and newspapers.

The Pottsville Republican stated, "After a month-long battle over which team won the Eastern Conference Southern Division title that (almost) ended up in the courts, a one-game playoff between the unbeaten Greyhounds and unbeaten Condors was ordered for Pottsville's Veterans Memorial Stadium".

There is also spectacular coverage in a special Saturday post-game December 7th, 1957 edition of *The Pottsville Republican*. My other source was the Monday December 9th, 1957 edition of *The Shamokin News-Dispatch*. Both differed slightly as to game accounts. Where there were differences, I went with my own eyes. I watched the game footage dozens of times. As with the previous game chapters, I also interviewed some of the players and included their recollections. Only this game evoked stronger emotions and clearer memories that have been etched into their brains.

It was a strange game; it was a frustrating game. It was not a thing of beauty. It was an ugly win for Cass, but it was still a triumphant win. Instead of three yards and a cloud of dust, this game was three yards and a face full of cold mud! The momentum shifted so many times, each team had to be dizzy.

Since you already know the ending, here are some things you may not know. On the field, the game was a muddy quagmire, and by game day, the frozen tundra of a football field had turned into a giant sea of mud. The ankle-deep, muddy field was speckled with white snow. On paper, the game was a statistical quagmire. Each team gained almost identical yardage on the ground. According to *The Pottsville Republican*, Cass ran for 229 yards to Shamokin's 227. Each team made exactly six first downs. Both fumbled exactly three times and recovered two of their three fumbles. And finally, both teams had the ball for 10 offensive series. Go figure! (*The News-Dispatch* reported different figures: Shamokin 131 yards gained to Cass' 141 yards, but the conclusion is the same - similar yardage for both teams.

There are two statistics where Shamokin actually "beat" Cass: passing (two completed) and interceptions (four).

First passing: the Greyhounds completed

two of their seven passes for a total gain of 55 yards (including a pass completed and one fumbled). Cass intercepted two of those seven. Cass threw the ball five times in the often torrential downpour. They completed no passes, but Shamokin alertly intercepted four of the five Cass passes. The Shamokin defense was great and thwarted Cass' offense many times, yet, ironically, Cass' defense won the ball game. One statistic where Cass won: weight advantage. Shamokin's line averaged only 158 pounds, Cass' about 180 pounds.

A disclaimer regarding accuracy on names used in this chapter is best said by the quote below directly from *The Shamokin News Dispatch* Monday December 9th edition:

> "Sports writers had a difficult job covering the contest because mud-spattered uniforms defied identification of players. Only personal knowledge scribes had of certain players' movements, stances and mannerisms enabled those in the press box to keep a reasonable good account of the game's progress."

So here we go: the very first Shamokin Greyhound to touch the opening kickoff from Cass' Ron Ney was Jerry Haupt. The same

Haupt you see on the cover photo was also the last Shamokin player to touch the ball when he punted.

The first series of plays (blurry, but note the *clean* uniforms) by both teams was uneventful, as neither was able to make the necessary yardage for a first down. However, Shamokin did something in this very first series that Cass would not do the entire game - they completed a forward pass. On the second play of the game, Jim Laughlin threw to Bill Wilson for five yards. This early in the game, you could still see the jersey numbers, so there is no doubt that three specific Cass defenders (Steve Kachmar, Joe Hydock, and Russ Frantz) all nailed Shamokin's passer for a loss before he could even set up to throw. Now on 4th down, Shamokin's Jerry Haupt had to punt. He barely got it off, as there was serious pressure by Cass' defense

After three short runs that went nowhere, Cass had to give up the ball. Gus Gressik had to catch the snap near his feet in the mud. This is the one snap all season that Dave Gauntlett was upset about. Cass' Gus Gressik punted "a beautiful punt" and pinned Shamokin inside its own 10-yd line, where Coach Pat wanted his much publicized defense to do what they did best, stop the other team in its tracks near their own end zone.

Shamokin could not move the ball. Cass held them to three yards and a "cloud of mud." When Haupt had to punt, the still fresh Cass defense rushed hard. This time the punt was partially blocked by Russ Frantz.

The Cass offense took over on their 34-yd line. With this great field position, Coach Pat had to be confident that his single wing offense could get Cass on the scoreboard early in the game. But it was not to be. After a few running plays, Harry Heffron threw the first of four Cass interceptions that day. In retrospect, some Cass players felt they should have kept the ball on the ground that rainy and cold day, where they might have scored a few times. But remember, Coach Pat and his guys liked to do the unexpected - pass when it looks like a run is in order and run when it looks like a pass. This time Heffron's jump pass was intercepted by Shamokin's Mike Strick near the Shamokin 30-yd line.

No panic though, as Cass still had Shamokin way back in its own muddy turf with 70 yards to go. Cass held the Greyhounds for another series. On 4ᵗʰ down, Jerry Haupt got off a great punt. Ryan caught it clean but fumbled during the runback. He recovered his own fumble.

Now Cass was back near their 30-yd line. Shamokin had succeeded in flipping the field. But after a few running plays, Cass had to punt it back to the Greyhounds. This time Gus got it off just in time and the ball rolled dead in the mud. Now Shamokin was back on their side of the field near their 37-yd line.

Shamokin controlled the ball for the next 12 consecutive plays. In this series, the 1ˢᵗ quarter ended. Shamokin ran the ball on every play but one, and that pass fell incomplete. Cass helped Shamokin with five free yards by jumping off sides. Shamokin stalled, Cass' defense held, and Shamokin punted near the 40-yd line.

The punt went over Ryan's head and into the end zone, so Cass had to start back at its own 20-yd line. See what I mean about a frustrating game? Punts, teams moving the ball up and down the field only to give up the ball. If you like defense and punting, this was your kind of ball game! Despite bad weather conditions and poor plays, both teams seemed composed, and remained focused.

Now it's time for a bit of excitement for Cass fans. After three short ground gains, Gus punted a nice, deep ball near midfield. Shamokin fumbled, and a muddy Cass player recovered. A gift! Cass continued the drive, including another jump pass by Heffron. This one fell incomplete, and Gus had to punt again.

Ken Hawk handled the wet ball, but he was immediately hit hard by Harry Butsko near the 30-yd line. Two more running plays went nowhere, so Shamokin made the mistake of calling a pass play. Jim Laughlin lost his grip on the soggy football and Weiner Antonelli picked it off to give Cass' offense another chance to score. There were now less than two minutes left in the first half.

Cass had the ball around its own 37-yd line. The Condors sure could use some momentum going into the locker room with a score. After a short gain, Cass called a tricky single wing play, a reverse pass. Wash Brennan tried to hit Russ Frantz near the goal line, but Shamokin's Henry Smith intercepted near the 5-yd line. Cass was thwarted again.

Less than a minute remained in the half, and Shamokin was on offense trapped back near its own 15-yd line. They called a timeout. Coach Lou Sorrentino decided to keep the ball on the ground in this risky area and ran the ball for two plays. Both plays *could* have been exciting, as the first run to the left resulted in the halfback getting tackled near his own goal line. On the second play, the Greyhound ball carrier could have broken loose, but did not. He gained over 10 yards as the clock ran out.

The muddy, wet players trotted into the warm, dry locker rooms. The fans headed for some hot coffee or chocolate. Here is a frustrating recap from the first half:

- ✓ 8 punts
- ✓ 4 fumbles
- ✓ 3 interceptions
- ✓ 1 completed pass
- ✓ 0 points scored

Wouldn't you like to hear what was said in those locker rooms? The coaches and players had to be pretty disgusted at the playing conditions. The Shamokin players were issued fresh white jerseys, but the Cass team was too poor to afford a *luxury* like an extra set of jerseys. So, to get the mud off, they did the only thing they could think of, they turned on the warm showers, and formed an assembly line. Each starting player, with his shoes still on, walked under as many shower heads as he could.

Meanwhile, Coach Pat was busy explaining adjustments that he thought would work in the 2nd half. He had no magic other than to encourage his strong defense to keep up the great work. And he praised his offense and stressed the obvious - ball control in wet muddy conditions. He knew they were trying their best.

And in the Shamokin locker room, Couch Lou and his assistants knew their boys were tired and a bit banged up in this, their fifth game in only three weeks. He was about 20 years younger than Coach Pat, but had produced a remarkable season in only his 2nd year coaching this team, and this was their 13th game! And under miserable playing conditions. (It was the 10th game of the 1957 season for Cass.) But Coach Lou and his brain trust planned a few trick plays you will read about soon.

There was an audible gasp from the fans as they saw "new" uniforms on both teams. What they did not know was the mud was washed off, but the Cass players were now even wetter than before. And now the chills had to set in as they ran out in the 39 degree cold late afternoon rain. Only the Shamokin Greyhounds had fresh dry jerseys. (Blurry photo shows clean white jerseys.)

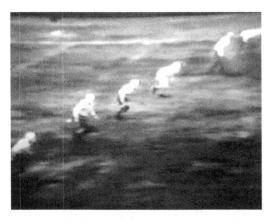

Both teams were focused and had to feel the importance of the next 24 minutes. For some, it would be the last time they would ever wear a football uniform. Few players would move on to the next level, college football.

It was Shamokin's turn to kick off. It went pretty far; however, Cass' Beakley Ryan was pumped up and ready to get the 2nd half going for Cass. He made a nice catch of the new dry football and returned about 20 yards. But Shamokin played as fresh as their uniforms looked, and they stopped Cass in its tracks. The Condors had to punt it away.

Gus punted high and deep, and Coach Lou had called his trick play on the return - a reverse. He must have used it here because the ball was still pretty dry, since the rain had let up a bit. He wanted to catch Cass sleeping. A reverse is where the return man, Jerry Haupt, caught the ball, ran sideways toward one side, and his teammate, Marlin Schickley ran the opposite way. Haupt handed the ball off to Schickley, and continued running, as if he still had the football. Cass was not asleep and hit him hard after a 15 yard return.

Now Shamokin had the ball for the first time in the 2nd half. After just one running play that yielded nothing, Shamokin quarterback, Jim Laughlin completed a nice pass to Don Tressler. Airing the ball early in the half was a seemingly smart thing to do. Except for one problem, the Cass defense! A few Condors hit Tressler so hard, the ball popped out and Gus Gressik recovered for Cass around the 26-yd line.

Cass now had a chance to gain the momentum with some great blocks by Steve Kachmar, Tony Phillips, Dave Gauntlett and the rest of Cass' offensive line. Weiner Antonelli made a great run near the middle of the line and ran all the way to the 10-yd line, no small endeavor with muddy feet.

It seemed like time to just pound the ball to the goal line, but after just one running attempt, Cass gained no yards. On the next run Cass again got nowhere against the strong Shamokin defense. As a bonus to Shamokin, a personal foul was called against someone from Cass, and the ball was moved back 15 yards. Now the ball was about 25 yards from the goal line. Coach Pat had used Harry Heffron's gifted athletic ability many crucial times during the season, as he had the unique ability to jump a few feet off the ground, and while in mid-air, throw a perfect pass to one of his receivers. This is simply called a jump pass. Not this time!

Shamokin's Mike Strick picked off the ball and made a nice return all the way to near mid field. So much for Cass' momentum. With only 10 yards to go for the go-ahead touchdown, Cass was back on defense near the 45-yd line.

As to momentum, Shamokin owned it now. They would have the ball for the next 15 straight plays, including the one that almost ruined Cass' historic season.

The Shamokin Greyhounds methodically moved the ball down the field. For nine straight plays, Shamokin ran the ball. They made first down after first down and ate up most of the 12 minutes of the 3rd quarter. By the 10th play of the drive, the mighty Cass defense was seemingly lulled into expecting only run plays. It makes sense, as why throw a pass now in the rain, and on a muddy field? Especially after you are driving on the ground with the momentum on your side. But Coach Lou used another trick play involving a pass.

This is likely the most controversial play in this significant playoff game, and one that some Cass' players still see in their nightmares. Shamokin completed a beautiful pass for what appeared to be a touchdown. It was 4th down with seven yards to go for a first down. First, a fake to Jerry Haupt, then a lateral from quarterback Jim Laughlin to his skilled halfback, Henry Smith. On this play the Cass defense was held at bay by the smaller Shamokin offensive line. Smith took his time, set his feet firmly, and fired off a perfect pass to Don Tressler in stride five yards from the end zone. A Cass defender, Harry Heffron was about five yards behind the receiver, and leaped in vain with outstretched arms into the mud. Tressler strolled in for what would have been the winning score for Shamokin. A perfect play except for one thing - a yellow flag!

Prior to the play, as Shamokin was set, their right halfback, Jerry Haupt, moved a split second before the snap. An alert official threw the flag for illegal procedure. No touchdown! The play did not count.

Allow me to put the controversy to bed. If you look at the play frame by frame, you will clearly see a flag appear in the upper frame long before Smith even got ready to throw. This was not a phantom flag, but a legitimate penalty because the Shamokin halfback moved. As you study this play, while the ball is in the air, you notice on the Cass sidelines, a figure wearing a hat running at full speed along the muddy sidelines. He was jumping up and down, apparently screaming at the officials. That was Coach Pat. He saw the illegal procedure, but likely did not notice that the head linesman had already thrown the penalty flag; he was just *politely* informing the officials there was a penalty. They knew, except for the one official back in the end zone with his arms in the air signaling touchdown. But no touchdown, and the ball was moved back five yards to the Shamokin 25-yd line.

Shamokin still had the ball, and Cass was not out of the woods yet. But it was 4th down and 12 yards to go, an obvious passing situation. (There were not too many field goals kicked in those days.) Good coaches run the ball when it looks like a passing circumstance, and that was exactly what Shamokin's leader called for, a run. Jerry Haupt, who was the goat on the previous play, as he caused the penalty, got handed the ball. He made a beautiful reverse run through the Cass defense all the way to the 10-yd line.

Now if you were a Shamokin fan, you thought your team was just robbed of a touchdown, but were not worried, as the football gods had given you another chance. It was first down and less than 10 yards for a score. After two runs, Shamokin had the ball on the 6-yd line, 3rd and six! So after 14 plays and being pushed to within six yards of their muddy goal line, do you think Cass was panicked? Not this Cass defense.

When Shamokin called for a run to its left side, Cass defense was ready. Big Harry Butsko crashed through and tackled the Greyhounds halfback Bill Wilson for about a 10 yard loss. It was 4th down and about 16 yards for a Shamokin touchdown.

Young Coach Lou Sorrentino loved the execution part of the 4th down trick pass play that was called back, so he called it again on 4th down. This time Smith had absolutely *no* time to set up. He was pressured by Tony Phillips and Charlie Zurat and a few others, and threw the ball up in the air. And it was caught near the 5-yd line! However, it was not caught by one of the Greyhounds, but was intercepted by a determined, ready, and angry Harry Heffron. The same Heffron who watched the ball sail over his head for an apparent touchdown a few plays ago. Harry ran strong and hard all the way to the 32-yd line. He was the ultimate team player, but was just as competitive as the next guy. Harry now had to feel relieved, as he achieved some form of football payback against Shamokin. The 3rd quarter ended with another huge momentum shift. Now it was Cass' turn.

Ironically, after Shamokin dominated the 3rd quarter clock with their 15 consecutive plays, it was Cass' turn to eat some 4th quarter clock. This sequence would prove to be the Cass offense's longest series of plays in the game - 11. The first five plays were old-fashioned Cass football, three yards and a face full of mud. The hard blocking of Kachmar, Gauntlett, Gressik, and Tony Phillips pushed the strong Shamokin defense back a few yards at a time.

On the seventh consecutive running play, Cass executed the wingback reverse to near perfection, perfect blocks and great ball handling. A fast Weiner Antonelli sprinted through the line for 45 yards all the way to the 10-yd line. Shamokin called a timeout.

The Cass fans had gone from being miserable, discouraged, and disheartened when Shamokin almost scored, to feeling elated. After all, they had seen the Cass defense save the day all season, and the Cass offense come through when it counted. They had to sense a score here. But it was not to be. The Greyhounds defensive line stiffened. After four running plays that got nowhere, including a 5 yard penalty against Cass, Coach Pat called a passing play. On a direct snap, Heffron threw the football toward the goal line. It may have been intended for Frantz, but a leaping Greyhound, Francis Verano, intercepted the ball. He ran it about 18 yards all the way back to the 20-yd line. Cass fans went back to being frustrated.

But this momentum for Shamokin players went nowhere, as they ensured Cass got another chance. After three runs for just a few yards, Jerry Haupt tried to punt Shamokin out of trouble. This time it was partially blocked by some muddy Cass defender. At this point and earlier, one cannot read jersey numbers, and the Cass team never cared who did it, the team did it.

This partial block was one of the key plays of the 4th quarter though because it kept the ball on the Shamokin side of the field. So now Cass fans had to be excited again because their team had the ball on the 36-yd line. It was 1st and 10 with less than five minutes left in the game.

After three short gains, all running plays, it was 4th down with only a yard to go. Surely Cass could keep the drive alive this time? They did, as Weiner Antonelli ran for about five yards for the first down. It was Cass' ball on the 18-yd line with less than four minutes on the clock. The score was still 0-0, but guess who had the momentum now! The Cass fans cheered.

Three more classic Cass single wing running plays, including a characteristic Beakley Ryan run for about nine yards, put the ball on the 10-yd line. After one more run up the middle that gained nothing, they called Weiner's number again. After all, it just worked four plays ago. Not this time. Antonelli plowed for five yards, and somehow lost control. Shamokin defense proved tough the entire game, and now they came through again. Ed Apollo recovered the ball for Shamokin on the 4-yd line. Whew! What an emotional roller coaster for fans from both sides.

With 90 seconds left, Shamokin had a first down and the ball in dangerous territory, their 4-yd line. The tension mounted. This time Cass must have really smelled blood. Their battle-scarred defense had one last shot at shutting down Shamokin and getting the ball back. Coach Lou had been burned before with passes in the rain, so he decided to keep the ball on the ground and not risk another Cass interception. Not where his team was, backed up near the goal line. Both he and Coach Pat knew Cass had only two timeouts left, so if the Greyhounds could get a first down, the game would end in a tie.

After a handoff up the middle went nowhere, Shamokin ran the ball on second down for just a one yard gain. This time Cass immediately called timeout. Now Cass had only one timeout left with 30 seconds remaining.

On 3rd down, Shamokin decided to keep it simple and quarterback Jim Laughlin handed the ball to Jerry Haupt, who gained about five yards to the 10-yd line. Cass - timeout! Now it was 4th down with only 15 ticks on the clock. Shamokin decided to punt the ball out of harm's way, knowing that Cass would likely get the ball back with only a few seconds left. After all, the way this game had been played, maybe a tie would be poetic football justice. These were two tremendous, proud defensive squads. But you already know what the final score is. Here is how it happened.

Shamokin lined up in punt formation, and time stopped. Tick tock! The ball was snapped, and as the seconds ticked away, the

Cass defensive line rushed with a fury, concentration, determination, and intensity known only to the most passionate of competitors.

No one was exactly sure what was going to happen. But Pat's team knew that somehow, someway, they had to block that punt. Shamokin's Jerry Haupt athletically handled the soggy, low-snapped football from his center. THUD! He punted it as hard as he could but Russ Frantz, Tony Phillips, Steve Kachmar, Gus Gressik, Harry Butsko, Joe Hydock, Charlie Zurat and the Cass defensive unit rushed like hell, as Pat would say!

Little did Jerry know that a Cass youngster, only in his junior year, Joe Hydock, a big kid, all of 205 pounds, would reach as high as humanly possible and cleanly block the football with part of his left hand, mere inches from the punter's extended right foot. As I stated before, bouncing footballs do strange things.

This one bounded right back toward Shamokin's end zone, and Russ Frantz, Cass team co-captain, tried desperately to grab the muddy ball before it rolled out of the end zone, for a touchdown. However, it rolled off his cold and wet fingertips and out of the end zone near a bank of piled up muddy snow. That was okay because a safety still counts for 2 points. The Cass players looked around and were stunned. No one was exactly sure what had happened or who even blocked the punt. They did not really care, as the scoreboard now read Cass: 2, Shamokin: 0! Everyone looked around. There were no penalties from the game officials.

Russ Frantz yelled out "Joey did it," meaning Joe Hydock blocked the punt. The fans, now all standing in the 40 degree rain, did not feel cold or wet, just shock and disbelief.

Essentially the game was over. But now, to add insult to Shamokin's injury, football rules state that "after a safety is scored, the ball is kicked off to the team that scored the safety from the 20-yd line." So Shamokin, down by two points, had to kick off to Cass with only a few seconds left.

The Greyhounds kickoff in the mud did not go very far, but it was indeed still a live ball and Cass had to handle it. Shamokin had to have desperate hopes of grabbing it and taking it all the way for a touchdown. But Beakley Ryan fell on the football and just lay there as the game ended. The fans, all standing in the cold rain, were either deeply dejected or wildly ecstatic. The players hugged, jumped up and down, and shook hands as they drifted toward the hot showers. Some players smiled, relieved that it was over. Many remembered that a nice prearranged banquet at a warm, dry place in nearby Minersville called "Deer Park" awaited both the winning and losing teams that evening.

Naturally, the Cass faithful were overjoyed, elated, proud, and happy beyond belief. And of course, Shamokin's Coach Lou Sorrentino, the players, coaches, and their fans were stunned and extremely disappointed. Their team had just played their hearts out, but had lost the championship with seconds remaining in the game. Cass knew in an instant that the team had done the impossible. But what they could not possibly know at that moment in time is that they had just become legends in Pennsylvania sports history. The 1957 football experience affected the rest of their lives. In the decades that followed, the Cass players and their coach formed a sort of mystic bond, and most remained friends for life and held many team reunions.

The playoff game itself certainly was a game of destiny, and one for the ages. A difficult game! As a footnote and in appreciation to the dedication to their craft, the officials deserve a huge note of appreciation: *Mr. Fillish (referee), Steve Martinec (referee or linesman?), Thomas Stenko (head linesman or field judge?), James Rettinger (field judge or umpire?), and Samuel Angle (alternate or umpire?). These men were the ones with the clean white (baggy) pants at the end of the game. They stayed upright in a field of mud and worked as a team. In this battle of punts and covering the entire field end to end, they called a flawless game. It had to be one they never forgot the rest of their lives. I know they were proud men for working that historic game.

By shear guts, great teamwork, and faith in each other and support from their community, Cass completed the entire season with a perfect record, scoring a total of 223 points to 0 by all opponents. UNDEFEATED UNTIED and UNSCORED UPON.

Unbelievable? It really did happen! And as the late Paul Harvey of radio fame used to say, "And now you know the rest of the story."

The Pottsville Republican and *The Shamokin News-Dispatch* listed the officials at different positions

Chapter 18

Post Season Glory

After the championship battle, the warriors from both sides of the muddy battlefield dined together. They had won each other's' respect. Immediately after the game both teams showered and changed into street clothes. The players and team officials jumped into the warmed up school busses and were taken a few miles to nearby Deer Park for a pre-arranged banquet together. Both teams! A few hours earlier, they were beating on each other in the cold rain on a muddy field. Now they sat side – by - side reliving the moments, discussing a historic game they would never forget.

One can only imagine the mixed emotions these players felt after the tremendous game they had just experienced. Cass Township had previously invited the Shamokin players and coaches to the dinner - regardless of the outcome of the playoff game. This was a great display of sportsmanship, especially considering the pre-game hype.

Remember the animosity between Shamokin's Principal Paul Swank and Coach Pat Droskinis earlier in the week? They argued at two conference meetings before compromising and agreeing to play each other. The

> "We salute Cass Township as Southern Division Champs."
>
> Paul Swank, Shamokin High School Principal

photo from the Monday edition of *The Pottsville Republican* showed a smiling Paul Swank handing the Southern Division trophy to Pat Droskinis at Deer Park. In between them - School Board President Jimmy Ryan and Cass team captain Russ Frantz. Looking on politely was a well-dressed young looking Shamokin Coach Lou Sorrentino.

To this day, Cass Township and its alumni are proud of their school and their sports teams. The Cass team was given the day off from school on the following Monday. They needed it.

The celebration did not end there. Some pomp and circumstance was in order a few months later. The University of Notre Dame head coach flew to Cass Township. The fighting Irish football coach, Terry Brennan was the guest speaker at Cass Township High School for their 22nd annual athletic banquet on February 4, 1958. Notre Dame just finished the 1957 season at 7-3 and was named to the top ten in the nation. Coach Brennan knew what it was like to be an underdog. He was the youngest major university coach ever when he was hired in 1954. He was only 25 years old. His first year, he coached Notre Dame to a record nine wins and only one loss. And the following year, 1955, Coach Brennan led the fighting Irish to an 8-2 record and was named coach of the year by the Washington Touchdown Club. Unfortunately 1958 would be the last year at Notre Dame for Coach Terry Brennan with a 6-4 record. Cass finished 1958 with

> Three players from Cass were named to Schuylkill County's 1957 All Star team - Russ Frantz, Ed Gressik, and Joe Hydock
> *The Pottsville Republican*

a 7-1 record, allowing only one touchdown.

Jimmy Ryan, Cass' School Board President, (above greeting Notre Dame coach Terry Brennan) served as toastmaster at the banquet. In the Cass tradition, it was not held in an extravagant rented facility, but in the high school gymnasium. Somehow they packed about 800 people into that small facility, which was decorated by the Cass student body.

For decades, the UNSCORED upon 1957 team was honored by *The Pottsville Republican*. They ensured that the Cass football team was not forgotten, especially on anniversary years like the 10th year, 25th and 50th. They published many articles highlighting the team's astounding performance. One of the best examples was on the 25th anniversary, December 7, 1982. Henry Kriner, sports writer for *The Pottsville Republican* wrote an entire page dedicated to the unscored upon team. It featured the large varsity team photo with names, and a nice picture of Coach Pat, proudly wearing his Cass

jacket, standing in front of his trophies and game ball (the picture on the dedication page). Henry encapsulated the entire perfect season with a game by game summary, complete with scores and dates. One of his headlines was "Pat had the horses." In the piece he highlighted the veteran line, mentioning each player by name. This article introduced the Southern Division champs to an entirely new generation, not yet born during the perfect season.

Sports writers like Walter Farquhar, Ronnie Christ, Henry Kriner, Art Follett, Charles Rose, Fred Zulick, John O'Connor, Willard Schraedley, and current sports editor Leroy

> "Pat had the horses." Henry Kriner, *The Pottsville Republican*

Boyer ensured new generations of sports fans knew all about Cass Township and the incredible football teams from 1957 and 1958. The photographers from the 1950s took some amazing action photos: Vince Ney, Bill Jacobson, Harry Folino, and Tom Wigoda.

Chapter 19

The School Board President

Jimmy Ryan

Everyone knew James "Jimmy" Ryan. He was the president of the Cass Board of Education for many years. Jimmy, as he was affectionately known, was so much more: he hosted three U.S. presidents. Mr. Ryan was a legend in Coal Country. He was a proud Irishman, a great guy who loved his school and lived life with a passion rarely seen. He was proud of the teachers and staff he had assembled at Cass: a few teachers were even Cass High graduates, and many were Kutztown State Teachers College ("University" today) grads.

Mr. Ryan was one of 12 children. He had to learn the value of hard work at a very young age. Everyone who knew him associated Jimmy Ryan with coal, but his professional life did not start out that way. Jimmy began working as a 13-year-old boy, a helper on a milk truck. Later in life, in the 1930s, he bought the very same milk route himself. As an entrepreneur, he expanded the concept and got into the trucking business, the ice business, and even delivered household goods and livestock to his rural customers. But, years later he always said, "The most profitable business was always ice." A simple concept, water is cheap, and ice is worth a lot more.

But coal was in the cards for Jimmy. He lived and worked in Schuylkill County, coal country. He used his trucks to deliver coal, and ended up building three coal breakers (huge buildings where coal is broken up and sized into various types). Two of these were Cass Contracting and Winne Land.

The political life was a natural evolution for a hard working businessman like Jimmy. He never really wanted public recognition, but it found him. His friendship was coveted by many and he became the Schuylkill County Democratic Party Chairman. He held on to that position for 25 years.

"Mr. Chairman", said President Truman to Jimmy Ryan. "I am delighted at the cordial reception you folks have given me."
President Harry S. Truman

Jimmy personally introduced three United States Presidents when they campaigned through the coal regions of Pennsylvania: Harry S. Truman in 1952, John F. Kennedy in 1960, and Lyndon Johnson in 1964. On October 21, 1952, Ryan greeted the first

sitting U.S. President to visit Pottsville, PA, President Harry S. Truman (see text box). He met the President, who was campaigning for a democratic presidential candidate, Adlai Stevenson, at Pottsville's train station. There was a crowd of about 15,000 folks there to greet the long Presidential campaign train.

So where is the Jimmy Ryan Presidential connection to UNDEFEATED UNTIED UNSCORED UPON, you ask? When President Truman addressed the 8,000 supporters waiting that October evening at Pottsville's Veterans Memorial Stadium, his first words addressed Mr. Jimmy Ryan, Chairman of the Schuylkill County Democratic Party. Just five short years later, Cass Township would play against Shamokin in that exact stadium.

> " Mr. Ryan Mr. Mayor, Governor Lawrence, Senator Clark, Congressman-to-be William Deitman, Ed Schlitzer, and Albert Nagle, ladies and gentlemen: I want to express my thanks to all of you ..."
> Senator John F. Kennedy

When Senator John F. Kennedy was running for president, he made a campaign address on October 28, 1960 in Pottsville, PA. A crowd of about 12,000 greeted him at Garfield Square. Democratic Party

Chair Jimmy Ryan was with Kennedy. His first words were to Mr. Ryan (see text box).

On August 21, 1961, then President Kennedy appointed Jimmy Ryan as a U.S. Marshall. Ryan was in charge of the Pennsylvania Eastern District, with headquarters in Philadelphia, PA.

In 1964, when President Lyndon B. Johnson was campaigning for re-election in the Northeast, he made a trip to Pennsylvania. Jimmy Ryan, still Schuylkill County Democratic Chairman, met his Presidential bus in Pottsville, and was invited to ride with him to a scheduled campaign stop in Allentown, PA. Ryan rode with the President as far as Schuylkill Haven. Because Ryan had a previous engagement himself, he asked the President if it was okay to get off the bus. Ryan's son, Sam, was following and took his father to his own commitment, a speech supporting the District Attorney in Reading, PA.

Jimmy Ryan maintained professional contacts at the local, county, state and federal level. Since Cass Township was a small school district, with a small tax base, they had a tough time budgeting. To ensure his athletic teams were able to even afford equipment, School Board President Ryan had to be creative. He was able to procure football helmets and other gear from the U.S. Naval Academy in Annapolis, MD. Jimmy had connections with a businessman in Pottsville, PA. His friend John Clark owned an Esso gas station there. Somehow, John was able to obtain surplus equipment from the Naval Academy. Jimmy appreciated the assistance from John (through tapping his network of connections). That was how things were done. Without those extra uniforms, especially the helmets, the Cass Condors may not have remained safe from serious injury.

Throughout his life, Ryan helped out those in need. Jimmy knew how to take care of people and things. During a

> **"Be nice to people and work hard."**
> Jimmy Ryan's simple motto for life

class in the fall of 1957, "teacher" Pat Droskinis noticed one of his students asleep in his chemistry class. It was one of his football players, Russ Frantz, so he did not yell at him too much. After class, Pat asked Russ, "What is the problem?" Russ explained that his house was cold since they ran out of coal to heat the house. He could not sleep too well in the cold. Pat went to see Jimmy Ryan, his "boss," and explained the situation. The next day, a truckload of coal was mysteriously delivered to the Frantz household. That was the kind of man Jimmy Ryan was, compassionate and generous! He did it anonymously.

Cass High School had state of the art stadium lights. The Cass Township Athletic Association purchased the Westinghouse lights in 1948 and paid for them in small installments. When Cass High School closed in 1966, and became part of the Minersville Area School District, Jimmy Ryan became the President of their Board of Education.

The Association sold the lights in 1969 to nearby St. Clair High School for under $20,000. By 1984, this investment had grown to $27,000. Back then, bonds paid as much as 13 percent. With coordination and business expertise, the Cass Township Athletic Association became a non-profit organization called the Cass Township Athletic Association Scholarship Fund. For 19 years annual awards totaling $3,000 were given to four graduating students from both Minersville High and Nativity High School. That makes a total of $57,000 given to 76 students from the sale of the lights. Jimmy Ryan passed away in 1982, but his spirit lived on in those Cass residents and graduates involved in the Cass Township Athletic Association Scholarship Fund he mentored and in whose values he promoted. A nice legacy for Jimmy Ryan

But the principal sum of money was still growing. After the awards were discontinued, there was still a balance of $65,000 remaining. At the annual Cass Township "all classes" reunion in 2008 and 2009 ten door prizes of $200 each were given to lucky Cass graduates. With a remaining balance of $61,388, the Cass Township Athletic Association Scholarship Fund committee decided to disperse all the funds. After all, the school closed in

1966 and the graduates and members of the committee were all in their 70s and 80s. The committee meticulously contacted as many living former Cass students as humanly possible. A daunting task. Under the leadership of Butch Condrack, the committee issued checks split among living Cass graduates.

The full committee is listed in the Epilogue, but if you look carefully, you will see a familiar name listed there, the center from the 1957 perfect season – Dave Gauntlett. Another familiar name appears - Jimmy's son James V. Ryan, Jr., known as "Sam." Sam was a 1958 Cass graduate, and a catcher on Cass' baseball team for three years. He played baseball with some of the same football players from the 1957 football season.

SCHUYLKILL COUNTY DEMOCRATIC COMMITTEE
404-405 Thompson Building
Centre & Market Streets
POTTSVILLE, PA.

James V. Ryan, Chairman
Peter V. McCloskey, Treasurer
Arthur Hummel, Secretary

Phone 622-8780

June 3, 1963

Mr. Pat Droskinas
Minersville, Pa.,

Dear Pat.

In Cleaning out our files we found these pictures that were taken at the Cass Twp. Banquet when Coach Terry Brennan from Notre Dame was our guest speaker.,
We thought you would like to have them.,
With kindest regards,

Sincerely

James V. Ryan

Chapter 20

The Captain

Russ Frantz

Russ Frantz was born Christmas Day, 1940, about a year before Pearl Harbor was attacked. He lived in Forestville, about a mile from Cass High School in a single-parent home, with a lot of kids in a small house. He was one of seven children raised by Edith, his mom. Edith was a well-liked, hardworking cook at Cass High School for years and then worked at the Minersville High School cafeteria after the districts merged. The kids were: Gladys, twins - Horace and Robert, Dorothy, Vivian, Herb, and Russ. His dad, Russell, left the family around 1945, when Russ was only 5 years old. All that Russ really cared to share is his father was a milkman in Mechanicsburg, PA and also worked at Indiantown Gap, a military installation. Two of the older sisters, Vivian and Dorothy helped out raising the younger ones. The twins both enlisted in the U.S. Navy and served in WWII, and Herb also joined the Navy and served during the Korean War. Herb retired from the Navy after 20 years of service, mostly on submarines. Robert was serving in the Pacific on a destroyer which was hit by the Japanese, and tragically, spent hours in the dark ocean. It is believed Robert suffered from this incident the rest of his life. He died way too young in his 40s.

Back to Russ. He was a nice guy and good kid. He was popular, but a bit on the shy side. He could have gone to either side of the tracks, but, thanks to sports, he had an outlet. And he used sports as that focal point for good.

He only lived about a mile from his high school. He rode the bus in the morning, but thanks to his athletic practices, walked home in the evenings. Russ was humble and played with focus, maybe to escape his sometimes tough private life. He was not just good at sports, he was a great athlete, who was a chiseled six feet three inches tall, and weighed about 190 pounds, pretty big by 1950s standards. Perfect for football, but it did not end there. Russ was a fantastic basketball player and one heck of a good left-handed baseball pitcher. His balance and nimble basketball skills surely helped him be a better football player. There was no track team at Cass, or Russ probably would have starred in that, too. He was the kind of leader who did not try to lead. He just did!

All the Cass kids knew Russ, but he was pretty selective about who he hung out with - mostly Harry, Gus, Weiner Antonelli, and his best friend Al Beretsky. Al was Russ's basketball teammate who graduated the year before Russ from Cass. When Russ accepted a football scholarship from Villanova, he was having self-doubts, as he was less than 200 pounds. Most of the guys on the line were about 230 to 240 pounds. Al encouraged Russ to stick it out, and said to him, "They don't always start the biggest guys, they start the best guys." Russ stayed!

In the summer of 1959, Russ was home on a weekend from Villanova. Al was a passenger and Russ was driving a 1950 Ford. Russ fell asleep and crashed over a steep hill. Al pulled Russ from the mangled car after that horrific accident. Russ had a badly broken and smashed femur and would never play another down of football again. In fact, Russ walked with a limp for the rest of his life.

He liked Sophia's, a local hangout and safe place located in Cass. It was also an escape from life and somewhere the teen-aged boys and girls could gather, their home away from home. They listened to the jukebox and laughed. Mostly, just clean fun.

Russ was a coach's dream, a natural athlete who would actually listen and let the coach help him be the best he could be. He was a polite boy and a born leader. The guys on the team liked and respected him and admired his tenacity. But perhaps he needed encouragement and a role model, because he and Coach Pat bonded. And Pat did not really know "how" to coach; like Russ, his captain, he just did it. Coach Pat, as a poor kid himself, also from a family of seven, and was a lot like Russ. He also came from an impoverished family, and used sports as his escape. Pat was also an end, like Russ, and knew more about that position than any other. He used to say, "If you can touch the ball, you can catch it!" And if Russ was near a ball, he sure did.

In those days one usually played both offense and defense, and Russ excelled at both. He was the team's leading scorer with 42 points that year. Individual statistics were not taken anywhere near today's standards, but Russ had more than a handful of interceptions and dozens of tackles. He was selected as a member of the PA all state team, quite an esteemed honor from such a small town, with only a small number of players on the team. The first year the facemask became a requirement was 1957. It was just a single plastic bar across the helmet. Russ had played three years without it, and, believe it or not, considered it a nuisance, because it interfered with his razor sharp vision.

Russ had played with and against some great ball players in the 50's. One of the greats was St Clair's Ed Sharockman, who went on to play 11 seasons in the National Football League with the Minnesota Vikings, and even play in one Super Bowl. Unbelievably, this team leader - this shy local hero, Russ Frantz, was just a mere 16-years-old, as he did not turn 17 until Christmas Day, 1957, when the football season was over and done.

Russ was among the few Cass athletes who played three sports: football, basketball, and baseball along with Weiner Antonelli, Gus Gressik, Harry Heffron, and Wally Brennan.

Russ Frantz was the first football player in the history of Cass Township to be named to the United Press (UP) PA All State football team in 1957. He was selected as an end. Later in life, he was selected for the Tubby Allen Rogowicz Schuylkill County Hall of Fame. He was inducted the same year as his high school basketball teammate Gene Horan; some Cass teammates, including Gary Collins, former NFL player, and Coach Pat Droskinis were in the audience.

Russ worked as an accountant for the Pennsylvania Turnpike for 38 years until he retired at the age of 58. He married Anne Hughes and together they had two children Russ and Lisa, both Penn State Graduates. Russ and Anne are very proud of their three grandchildren, also all college graduates.

Chapter 21

The Quarterback

Wash Brennan

The guys called Walter Brennan "Wally," Coach Pat called him Walter, but he liked the nickname Wash best. Brennan also was called Wowie and Pal by his family. Most importantly, he was called into action as the quarterback as a result of Ted Wannisky's season ending broken collarbone in the second quarter during the fifth game on Oct 10th when Cass beat Ashland's Black Diamonds 19-0 on their home turf. Wash played quarterback on offense and safety on defense, and was only a sophomore.

Brennan was an interesting guy: he was only in 10th grade, and weighed about 145 pounds and was all of 5 ft. 9 inches tall. He was born on June 17th, 1941 and unknown to his team mates, he was just as old as the juniors and seniors were, 16! He held himself back in grade school when unknown to his parents, he actually "quit" first grade while attending St Kieran's Catholic School because he was not ready for school. Of course he had to repeat first grade, but the next year went to Glen Dower Public School, Foster Township.

Up to the October '57 season, Brennan mostly played jayvee football and substituted a bit for the varsity, when Cass had a good lead. He was also the varsity extra point holder taking those perfect snaps from Dave for Frank Machita to kick. Coach Pat told him after the Ashland shutout, and Wannisky injury, "No more jayvee stuff for you Walter, you just got promoted to varsity!" Brennan went on to play two more football seasons, and led the Cass Condors to another almost "perfect" season in 1958. He led his team to five more consecutive shutouts until Mahanoy Township finally scored on Oct 23, 1958. Cass only allowed one touchdown in 15 consecutive games at that point! After this loss, Brennan regrouped, showing his character, and led Cass to two more unscored upon games in 1958 to finish his junior year with a record of seven wins and one loss. He was part of the two-year historic run where Cass only allowed one team to score points in a total of 18 football games!

During his senior year in 1959, Brennan continued playing quarterback, but without the help of the six seniors from the previous season, who had graduated. They included big star ends, Gene Horan, as well as Harry Butsko, who went on to play in the NFL with the Washington Redskins in 1963. Cass' record dropped to 3 wins, 4 losses and 1 tie.

Interestingly, Brennan was the only Cass player to follow Coach Pat's career path of both teaching and coaching football. Wash went to Penn State University and received his Bachelor of Arts Degree in Social Studies in 1965. He got his first teaching job, albeit brief (1965-1966), at Landover High School in MD. He accepted a teaching position at Williams Valley High School, PA, later that same year, 1966, because it included an assistant football coaching position.

But after only one year, Brennan took a two-year break from Williams Valley in 1968-69 and went back to Penn State. He earned his Master's Degree in Earth Science in 1969. Williams Valley must have still liked Coach Brennan, as he was offered the head coaching position in 1969. He accepted the offer, and left Penn State "Happy Valley." Brennan even tried to employ the single wing offense that he learned at Cass. He was even mentored by his old friend, Coach Pat on single wing offense. However his center was not a "Dave Gauntlett" perfect snapper, so it did not work out. He used single wing offense for only one game. He then used a more traditional wishbone offense and it worked. His team was very successful and they won their first championship in 1970.

Brennan accepted an assistant coaching job in 1972 at Minersville, his former rival, which by now had merged with his beloved Cass. He helped Minersville win the Schuylkill County championship. Next, in 1973, after the head coach resigned, Coach Wash was promoted to that position.

He coached in Minersville from 1973 to 1975, and maintained his winning ways. Coach Wash won a few trophies for the mantle as he won his second Schuylkill County championship in 1973 with an 8-3 record. His team improved in 1974 and won the Class B Eastern Championship with a 9-2 record. In 1975 with an in 8-2-1 record, he again won the Schuylkill County championship. Brennan was well-liked by his players and peers.

On the same weekend of his Cass High School Reunion in 2008 celebrating the unscored upon season as a player, Coach Brennan was recognized as a championship coach by Williams Valley High School at halftime of their football game. But, similar to Coach Pat's early success as a coach, Brennan would never again match his amazing record coaching at Williams Valley and Minersville.

In 1976 he moved to Wildwood, NJ, and coached only two more years as a head football coach. His team only won one game that first year and lost seven. The second year in 1977 was not much better as they only won two games and lost six.

But he still had a passion for working with youngsters, so he coached in the 1980s as an assistant coach in football, baseball, and track.

During his teaching and coaching career, teachers did not make enough in salary to raise a family so most worked summer jobs. Wash was an interesting hard-working guy and a master of versatility. He worked dozens of different summer jobs, everything from driving a bus, construction, selling diamond rings to managing an Officer's Club at Ft Indiantown Gap, PA.

He retired from teaching in 1998 to settle in Egg Harbor, NJ with his wife Judy Russian. In 2017 and at the time of this first edition, they have been married over 52 years. They have three children, Sean, Terrance, and Shannon-Marie. He and Judy have four grandchildren – all girls .

Here is a direct quote from the now retired Mr. Brennan about those magical Cass years:

"The team was a group of great young men who grew to be outstanding citizens, parents, grandparents and friends who knew how to win. They were blessed with ability and natural strength of muscle, heart and soul. God brought them together to raise the spirit of many parents who worked hard and sacrificed much at that time and that place. I should not be singled out for the small part I played in their lives, and I thank them for letting me share those moments when we were invincible."

Chapter 22

The Future NFL Player

Harry Butsko

Harry Butsko was only a 16-year-old junior for the magical 1957 season, so he had the opportunity to play one more year for Cass. And what a senior year he had. He was the team captain for the 1958 season that continued the unscored upon tradition for five more games. That is a total of 15 straight games where Cass held all opponents scoreless, and Harry was a big part of every one of those games. Except for one single pass play on Oct. 23, 1958, where Mahanoy Township scored, Harry would have been part of a team that would have gone two entire seasons holding all opponents scoreless.

Butsko finished his senior year leading the Cass team to seven wins and only that one loss. The United Press International (UPI) selected Butsko to the first team on their "All State Pennsylvania" high school football team. In fact, he played in what was called the "Big 33 All-Star Team." At the time this was like a super bowl for high school players. That Pennsylvania team played against the All Americans (from all around the country) in Hershey, PA in late summer in 1959. We "zapped them, we really whipped up on them," Harry emphatically stated, during an interview. Of course it was a shutout, continuing the unscored upon tradition, 18-0.

He also played with his Cass teammate, Frank Machita, on the Dream-Team which was a high school All-Star team game that benefitted crippled children. It was played at Pottsville Veterans Memorial Stadium on Dec 4th, 1958, the same stadium where they both had played in the rainy, muddy Shamokin championship game one year earlier (Dec 7th, 1957). But again, extremely horrible weather affected the game, for both fans and players. This time it was snow, and thick pea soup fog. Since the grass was covered with an inch of white snow, it was lined with black coal dust. But when the eerily thick fog rolled in, the fans could not even see the playing field. Only the players, officials and maybe those close to the sidelines could actually see the game.

Harry really loved playing defense. When asked why, he smiled and said, "I'd rather hit people than be hit!" That may explain his passion for playing defense, and why he was offered a football scholarship by the University of Maryland.

Remember earlier in Chapter 3, when Harry said "We were all so poor, even the poor kids called us poor?" A scholarship was the only way Butsko was able to escape poverty, and could afford to go to college.

Though he was recruited by Maryland Assistant Coach Lee Corso to play as an end, Harry showed his Cass team spirit, and pure love of the game, and played college ball in any position needed: center, tackle, fullback, or linebacker.

But his favorite place on the football field was playing linebacker. In college, he had bulked up to about 210 pounds, but was still quick, and that position gave him the best opportunity to do what he loved, hit the ball carrier. His favorite play at Maryland happened in 1961. He nailed a Penn State quarterback, Galen Hall, for a seven yard loss, when Penn State was threatening on the 2-yd line, with the score 21-17. That day, the Maryland Terps became the first Maryland team to beat Penn State by a final score of 21-17.

Harry was proud to be an integral part of what the defensive players of the Maryland Terrapins called themselves that year, the Gangbuster Defense. He played a bit of offense but never scored a college TD. A good friend of his did score, many times - Gary Collins. In high school, while Harry was playing for Cass, Gary played for nearby Williamstown. Gary went on to play almost a decade of NFL football for the Cleveland Browns. Harry and he remain lifelong friends.

During his college career (Harry received his BS degree from Maryland in 1963), he must have caught the eye of more than a few NFL scouts. He was drafted by both the San Diego Chargers of the American Football League, and by the Washington Redskins of the National Football League in the 15th Round. He accepted a $1,000 signing bonus and $9,500 salary from the Redskins, a lot of money back in the 1960s. He signed and reported to training camp in June 1963. For the first time in his life, he was not poor. He celebrated by buying a 1963 Ford 500 XL convertible.

Harry Butsko
52 Linebacker - Redskins 1963

During the 1963 pre-season games, Harry got a chance to show that he belonged in the NFL. He played in most every pre-season game, and made it on the final 39 man roster. But there was some hard work and harder fun in pre-season camp. Harry recalled one special moment where the veteran players "asked" him and the other rookies to stand up on the dining room table and sing their college fight songs. This was long before karaoke, so no words appeared on the screen (what screen?), so he made them up!

Harry hustled at all times, and was versatile. He was a total team player, so the Redskins decided to use him in his rookie season exclusively as a special teams player - kickoffs, kickoff returns, punting and punt returns. On a historical note, when JFK was assassinated on Nov 22, 1963, the NFL considered cancelling all their games that weekend, but decided against that. Two days later, the Washington Redskins played against the Philadelphia Eagles. Harry was on that football field.

That one year as a pro, he had the unique opportunity to play with and against some of the greats - two of his more well-known teammates were Ben Davidson and Norm Snead. Harry played against Sam Huff, Sonny Jurgensen, and Mike Ditka.

Harry was the youngest of 11 children, born to Ukrainian immigrant parents Anna and Alex Butsko on Feb 2, 1941. However, he was not the first of the 11 to go to college: his older brother, Frank, attended the U.S. Naval Academy in 1956, where he played solid football all four years. After graduation, Frank was commissioned a lieutenant in the Marines, and served two tours in Vietnam. In fact all seven of Harry's brothers served in combat. Prior to Frank serving in Vietnam, there were Peter, Andrew, Steve, and John who served in WWII. Metro and Paul followed, and both served during the Korean War.

A little known fact is that Harry Butsko also served his country in the Army Reserve and the National Guard. After playing one full season of NFL football with the Redskins in 1963, he put on a different uniform - that of a soldier. He joined the National Guard and attended basic training at Ft Jackson, SC. Now all eight Butsko brothers had honorably served their country.

When he returned to the Redskins from Army duty in the summer of 1964, he was a quite a bit heavier at over 230 lbs. and must have lost some quickness. He also hurt himself during the preseason on a kick off against the Baltimore Colts and was placed on injured reserve. That was the beginning of the end of his NFL career. He was traded by the Redskins to Denver. After only a few weeks with the Denver Broncos, they sent him to the San Diego Chargers, where he never even got a chance to practice and was unceremoniously cut from the team. Coach Sid Gilman, the same coach who had drafted him in the 15ᵗʰ round the previous year, likely did not appreciate that Harry decided to go with the Redskins.

But Harry, though he married his college sweetheart Joy Limerick in 1964, was not yet ready to give up on football. He went on to play for the Edmonton Eskimos in Canada for only about a month, then returned to the USA and played in the Continental Football League. He chased his pro football dream for a while, playing in 1964 in West Virginia for the Wheeling Ironmen and again in 1965 in Connecticut for the Hartford Charter Oaks. In 1966 he even asked his old team, the Washington Redskins for a

tryout, but Redskins coach Otto Graham cut him.

When the Lord called, Harry answered. He grew up as a Catholic, and fully accepted Christ as his Savior at age 30. He was attending mass with his mother-in-law at the Nazarene Church, Capitol Heights, MD. He states that at that moment, he really understood the significance of a relationship with Jesus.

"The most important thing in life is not football. It is the acceptance of Christ as Savior and Lord."

Harry Butsko

Harry applied for and was offered a position with the United States Post Office as a Public Relations Officer. During that time, he lived in Upper Marlboro, MD, and worked as the Postal Congressional liaison for Capitol Hill. He retired after 28 years of service. He and his wife had three children and four grandchildren. After retirement from the Postal service, he and Joy moved to Duncannon, PA in 1995. They still live there at the time of this printing.

Gene Horan and Harry Butsko at a Cass Reunion in 2008. They were the starting ends for the Cass football team in 1958.

Chapter 23

Coach Pat's Life

More Than a Coach

Peter John "Pat" Droskinis was born on June 2, 1915, the second of nine children born to recent Lithuanian immigrants Casimir and Anna Droskinis. When the Russians invaded Lithuania, they forced young boys to serve in the Russian Army. Pat's father, Casimir, was lucky. About to be inducted, he escaped in 1907 to Scotland where he learned coal mining as a vocation; he was recruited as a coal miner, and boarded a boat to America a few years later. Minersville, PA must have sounded like the right town in which to settle, especially since there was a growing Lithuanian community in New Minersville.

Pat really loved a quote from Booker T. Washington's *Up From Slavery* (see text box) and frequently referred to it in his banquet speeches. Indeed, as did Booker T. Washington, so did Pat have more than his share of obstacles in life. But so did the kids at Cass. Perhaps that's why they formed such a bond on the ball field and later

> "I have learned that success is to be measured not so much by the position that one has reached in life as by the obstacles which he has overcome while trying to succeed,"
> Booker T. Washington, in his book, *Up From Slavery: An Autobiography.*

in life, a brotherhood of sorts.

Life was tough in Minersville for a near penniless immigrant family that spoke Lithuanian with little English. Pat's father had to work long hours in the coal mine and the family got by on next to nothing. Pat was actually held back in first grade. Not because he was unintelligent, but because he hardly spoke any English! Ironically, he was sent home to learn English, as the teachers were not aware of his family's background.

But Droskinis was a fast learner, and quickly adapted to school and hard times. Life in the 1920s may have been "roaring" in the big cities, but not for the poor coal miners and their families in Pennsylvania. Pat remembers picking berries after school so the younger kids would have something to eat. He also helped out any way he could, picking unburned coal from dumps to heat the house, cutting wood and carrying it miles to his home, and picking wild mushrooms for soup.

His home life was far from idyllic! A tough home life, his father was an alcoholic and

> In junior high, Peter Droskinis and his friends watched games at Minersville Park. They each picked a player and followed his play. He picked "Patsy Eagan", from Mt. Laffee. After that he became known at Patsy or Pat

often would beat his mother. Only 10 years old, young Pat once had to stop his father from such spousal abuse by punching and knocking his father out. In the process, his own father accidentally knifed him on the wrist. "Blood flew to the ceiling," Pat wrote in "Coal Miner's Son" (unpublished memoirs). It's not surprising that Pat felt the need to counsel his athletic family, the boys at Cass Township High School. He wanted to show them the kind of proper love and mentoring he rarely received.

When the Great Depression hit the country in the 1930s, Pat stated that he remembered his whole family going to soup lines in Minersville with pails in hand. Yet somehow the Droskinis family survived those hard times. To make matters worse during his junior year, Pat's father was laid off from his job at a coal mine in Buck Run. The family continued to struggle tremendously.

As a teenager Pat had to find a way to cope. In high school he used sports as a form of temporary escape from poverty: Pat lettered in baseball, track, football, and basketball. Pat mentions an ironic sports highlight in his memoirs. He hit the only home run of his high school career for Minersville in 1932, a walk off homer to win the game. The team he was so proud to beat – Cass Township!

Many towns and churches fielded their own semi-pro sports teams back in those days. During high school Pat made a few dollars playing for "St. Vincent's" against some other local teams: the Minersville Wildcats, the Mahoney City Brewers, and others. In basketball, he played for the "St. Francis Juniors" against such teams as The Russian's Shoe Five, and the Llewelyn All-Stars. Pat's true love must have been baseball. He played for multiple

teams, as stated in his memoirs: New Minersville, Seltzer City, Oak Grove, Pine Grove, Felsburg's, and the Minersville Senators, among others.

He was also an excellent student, receiving mostly A's and B's and graduated *cum laude*. Not bad for a kid that got held back in first grade!

He even sang in plays and operettas. On June 6th, 1933, less than a week after his 18th birthday, Droskinis also tried his hand at

acting, playing King Arthur in the Minersville graduating class play called "The Knight's Mare".

After graduating from Minersville High in 1933, Pat worked as a short order cook working 6PM until 2AM at a local restaurant in Minersville called "Perry and Shad's" (later became "Felsburg's"). His pay was a mere $1 per day, seven days a week, and free food. I guess it beat working underground in the mines. The restaurant gave him time off to play on the semi-pro sports teams.

Here is a mystery I am unable to solve about my father. He was offered a football scholarship, but did not begin college for two years after his 1933 high school graduation! I am certain he continued playing semi pro sports to supplement his $1 per day cook's pay.

It was not until 1935 that he accepted his athletic scholarship at Kutztown State Teachers' College (now University). His coach was James F. MacGovern. As a freshman, Pat started on the varsity football, basketball, and baseball teams. Pat also began his decades long officiating career while at Kutztown. He called local sandlot football games for $1 per game. Halfway through the 1935 fall football season, the Kutztown athletic department must have been in a financial crunch. The college president, Dr. Rohrbach, called Pat and the other MacGovern recruited players to his office. They were told to "pay $300 or leave," according to "Coal Miner's Son." This was a tough blow for Pat because he only had $100 saved. However, thanks to the kindness of Professor Allan Bubeck, one of Pat's teachers, he was able to continue. Mr. Bubeck (Psychology) loaned Pat the extra $200, and this young student athlete was able to finish his freshman year.

What a year Droskinis experienced. The Kutztown basketball team, under Coach MacGovern, won the Pennsylvania State Teachers Colleges championship with an 11-2 record. (The assistant coach was Bill Eberts, from Cass Township) Remarkably, Droskinis would not return to Kutztown as a sophomore until 1947 after serving in the Army and being able to use the GI Bill! Back in Minersville in 1936, his family was suffering through the depression and Pat felt obliged to return and help out. Even his sister Connie was working in a local factory and his brothers were all working with their father in the mines.

For the next eight years he worked in the coal mines with his dad and brothers. Places with strange names like Red Stripes, Buck Mountain, Big Hill, Little Diamond Vein, and Froggy's. He got hurt plenty of times. Once a sliver of coal was stuck in his eye, another time he stepped on a large rusty nail and pulled it out himself with a pair of pliers. The years in the mines did not dampen his love of sports. After a hard day's work, Pat found happiness by playing semi-pro sports with distinction and secretly dreamed of a better life. Plus he was being paid as a semi-pro, and that helped.

Mining coal was and is a dangerous business. On a freezing cold December day in 1940, Pat nearly died in a horrible coal mining accident. He was working with his dad and his brother, George, who was home on leave from the U.S. Marine Corps. They drove their old Buick Special out to the coal shaft, and jacked it up on blocks. They removed a wheel and bolted a special homemade pulley onto the drum. With the Buick idling, they used the device, a long 100 foot metal cable attached, to hoist a buggy with over a

ton of coal from the deep shaft up to the surface. Pat was topside, near the cable and somehow, it caught his pants and pulled him under the huge Buick.

It got worse. As the cable was winding onto the drum, Pat was trapped and the cable pulled his clothing and his leg into the drum. If Pat could not stall out the car's engine, he would be killed: the buggy might come to the surface and landed on him. Again and again he used a long metal pole to try to stall the car. It did not work, but as the coal buggy surfaced the car engine finally stalled. Pat was saved. He screamed, hoping his dad or brother, 100 feet below the surface, would hear him. They did not.

Somehow, near naked, frozen and bleeding, Pat struggled to the mouth of the mineshaft and called for help to his father and brother below the earth. Just then, the cable broke and the buggy, loaded with a ton of anthracite coal, knocked Pat underneath. The buggy and Pat plummeted below. He was unconscious, but alive. George and his dad must have been shocked seeing a full buggy with Pat under it, plummeting down the mineshaft. George's United States Marine Corps training kicked in: with superhuman strength, he somehow freed Pat from the buggy and carried him to the surface. As the cold hit Pat, he regained consciousness and George gently laid him in the backseat of the car. After taking a layer of his own extra clothes off, George put them on Pat and immediately put the wheel back on the Buick.

They took Pat to the hospital. Though the wounds

> "I was cleaned up and patched up all over – head, arms, body. I looked like a wrapped up mummy."
> Pat Droskinis, coal miner

were deep, they were not life threatening. Pat spent a week in the hospital. Recuperating at his parents' home for 30 days, Pat resumed his mining career in the same mine he was injured. Pat worked in the coal mines for another four years. George returned to the military life with his other brothers – the Marines.

Tragically, George and Pat would never see each other again. George was assigned to combat duty in the Pacific Theater. He made the ultimate sacrifice. He was attached to the U.S. Army's 38th Division in combat in Luzon, the Philippines. USMC Private First Class George Droskinis was cut down by machine gun fire while saving another Marine. George was posthumously awarded the Silver Star for his heroics.

During WWII Pat and his five brothers (Joe, Victor, George, John and Billy) put their lives on hold and served their country. Pat was the last to serve. He was drafted by the U.S. Army in March 1944. Before he reported to active duty, Pat married his girlfriend of about six years, Dorothy "Dot" Schneck. Dot, from Pine Grove, PA, was also raised in a home where no English was spoken. Her grandmother raised her and only spoke Pennsylvania

Dutch, a dialect of German. Pat and Dot spent the rest of their lives together.

Pat never served in combat. By the time he was ready to deploy from Ft Belvoir, VA, the war ended. Sports in his veins, Pat spent the remaining time of his service officiating basketball games on post. He even played Army baseball and basketball, and he still mined coal. Every other weekend, he drove from Ft Belvoir, VA to Minersville, PA and opened a coal mine with his brother, Joe. During this time, Pat became a dad! My older sister Dawn was born in November 1945.

The war afforded a new lease on life for Pat. He used the GI Bill to resume his college career as a sophomore at Kutztown, at age 32! Veterans from WWII also received $20 per week for 52 weeks, and Pat earned extra money doing what he knew best – he officiated and played semi pro football. His favorite highlight: at age 34, he was the starting end on the semi-pro Pottsville Maroons in 1949. They won the Eastern Division Pennsylvania State Championship.

Pat was a husband, a father, and a semi-pro football player while attending Kutztown from the fall of 1947 until he graduated in 1950. He also got his first opportunity to coach. He was an assistant football coach in 1949 under head coach Joe Patton.

In 1950 as a 35 year-old college graduate, he began teaching and coaching at Minersville High School. Prior to that, he experienced very tough times. His hard work was finally beginning to pay off - he was a teacher at the same small high school he had graduated from 17 years earlier. Pat was offered a physics and chemistry teaching position for $2,000 per year. He started in February 1950, and finished out the remainder of the school year. In the 1951-52 school years, he also would become head basketball and baseball coach, which bumped his annual salary up to $2,400, closer to the national average salary of $3,200.

It did not take long for Coach Pat to experience some glory in his hometown. In 1952-53, Droskinis was the head coach of the first Minersville basketball team to win the South Schuylkill league championship. They averaged 70 points per game, and had a win loss record of 22-5. (That is seven-year-old Dawn Droskinis in the picture with her dad.) Pat had some great players because Minersville school district had just absorbed the smaller Branch

Township. The team's star players were Al Quinn, Don Hauser, Herm Huntzinger, and Bob Doyle. Under the "irony" category, Minersville beat Pine Grove in the playoff game March 2, 1953, (65-61). Droskinis would become Pine Grove's assistant principal and athletic director 20 years later.

On a personal note, I was born during that 1953 basketball season. Since February 12 is Lincoln's birthday, the basketball players wanted my parents to name me "Abe." Glad they did not.

During the 1950-1954 summers, Droskinis earned his master's degree in education from Temple University in Philadelphia. Pat already had already experienced the value of earning his bachelor's degree to escape the coal mines. He knew a master's degree would help him further his teaching career and earn a better salary to support his growing family.

As Pat was finishing his master's degree in 1954, the Cass head coach, Sandy Phillips, resigned. Cass Township High School was in a real bind because Phillips not only coached all sports, but also was a chemistry teacher, an unusual combination. Where could Cass find someone with these uncommon credentials? Pat Droskinis fit the bill!

Cass School Board President "Jimmy" Ryan offered to double Pat's salary to a whopping $5,000 a year, if he agreed to coach all sports and teach science and chemistry at Cass. Pat was hesitant at first since Cass was very small and had a small tax base. They were already having trouble paying their existing teaching staff. Jimmy sealed the deal with Pat when he guaranteed his salary "even if I have to pay you out of my own pocket," said Ryan. In those days a handshake was all that was needed. Jimmy must have seen into the future. No one dreamed of the sports history that was in the making at Jimmy's beloved Cass.

It was a good fit. My dad once told me he believed it was divine intervention, in bringing this team together with him at the right time and right place. When Pat played college and semi-pro ball, he functioned as a player-coach on the field, especially when he was still playing after age 30. So naturally as a head coach, he still had the ability to think like a player, which gave him a definite edge motivating the guys from Cass. He was an innovator, a shrewd judge of talent and an excellent teacher and coach - and the guys responded to Pat's approach and discipline. They proved to be a once in a lifetime group of players.

Droskinis was not just a Cass football coach. Note his successful record in basketball and baseball below:

	Football	**Basketball**	**Baseball**
1954	2-5-1	6-8	10-4
1955	4-5-1	8-6	8-6
1956	7-2	9-5	7-5
1957	10-0	10-4	10-1
1958	7-1	17-6	11-2
1959	5-2		

Coach Droskinis had amazing years at Cass. He was in his prime as the head coach in all sports, and was the science and chemistry teacher. The years 1954 through 1959 were magical in Coach Pat's life. He was living the American dream – he had his own home, a car, a good salary, a family and he only had to drive two miles to work.

By 1959, Pat saw the declining enrollment at Cass, so he was open to offers. Nearby Schuylkill Haven had a chemistry teaching position open and offered Pat the job. Since it was a larger school within driving range and included a pay raise, Pat accepted. However, he stayed at Cass and coached the Cass football team to a winning season in 1959, and then transitioned that October to Schuylkill Haven. He also agreed to be Coach Harry Hummel's assistant football coach at Schuylkill Haven. Pat had an expanding family now, as his third child was born, John (now Jon), in October 1960.

When Hummel left Schuylkill Haven in 1962, Pat became the head football coach. It was not the same atmosphere of success and local fame he experienced at Cass. Not even close. In his four years as Schuylkill Haven's head football coach, Pat produced a mediocre win-loss record.

As head basketball coach for only one year, Pat had a glimpse of "Cass glory." His 1962 team had a great year. They played against Minersville only to lose the championship game in the final 30 seconds. The Minersville team was coached by Tom Fitzpatrick.

Somewhere around 1965, Droskinis was offered an assistant coaching job at Wilson High School with his old friend, coach John Gursky (former Minersville coach). He actually accepted and only reneged when the Schuylkill Haven administration offered him a raise. Ironically Pat was fired the following year as Schuylkill Haven head football coach. Gursky went on to glory as a longtime coach at Wilson.

At Pottsville in 1966-67, Pat was assistant football coach and assistant track coach. He only stayed for one year. A highlight: One of his star players was Jack Dolbin, who went on to play in a Super Bowl for the Denver Broncos. In his memoirs, Pat states "Dolbin did not need my advice or coaching." Working as a coach at Pottsville's Veterans Memorial Field had to be a strange feeling for Pat. Remember, just a decade earlier this was the exact football field on which his beloved Cass team had won the Shamokin playoff game. He had to smile once in a while about these feelings.

The phone rang at Pat's home in the summer of 1966. It was Jimmy Ryan, now the president of the Minersville School Board of Education, calling to offer him a chemistry teaching position in Minersville. Pat accepted, even though he would not be the head football coach. Droskinis would be the assistant coach to Terry

Case. Jimmy Ryan hired Pat Droskinis for the *second* time in his career.

Halfway through the football season, Coach Terry Case resigned. Pat Droskinis had become the head football coach in the same hometown high school he graduated from 34 years prior. Unfortunately, when he took the reins after five games, the team had not won a single game. Coach Droskinis did no better than Coach Case. Minersville finished the season with a 0-10 record. Exactly the opposite of his Cass 10-0 record a decade earlier.

On a personal note, it was an interesting time for me. I shared quarterback duties that year on the Minersville freshman football team with Robert "Scoop" Kumpaitis - and my dad was the head football coach. When jayvee quarterback Joe Balsis, Jr. (son of the world championship billiard player) broke his ankle, Scoop and I got a chance to play jayvee football. Between us we weighed only 200 pounds, but the team actually won a few games.

It seemed the magic had returned the following football season (1968) when Minersville won the first two games undefeated and unscored upon. My dad was motivated again. That was the end of the fairy-tale though, as the varsity lost the remaining eight games. It still seemed exciting for me, as I made the varsity squad and was

backup quarterback to Joe Balsis and Joe Butensky. My head coach was also my dad, and I remained hopeful and optimistic. One of my teammates was Newtown's John Zernhelt, who went on to become a head college coach and an assistant NFL coach for both the NY Jets and the Tennessee Titans.

The 1969 season was the last year Coach Pat ever would coach football. We won only two games and lost eight. It seems Coach

Pat had not changed his coaching style but the 1960s were not the 1950s. The times had changed, though Coach Pat had not. We reflected our 60s heritage and were not like the unselfish guys from Cass. Coach Pat could no longer relate to his players and bond, as he did in the 1950s. There were some great players, but we were not a great team. The discipline was gone. Coach Pat was fired before the 1970 season began.

Chemistry teacher (not coach) Droskinis remained at Minersville through 1973. It had to be tough on him as he watched his replacement, Coach Charlie Zontanos, come in from Arizona. Two seasons later, Coach "Z" as he was affectionately known, lead Minersville to a championship in 1971 with a 10-1 record.

Pine Grove High School needed an assistant principal. When this opportunity to move into administration came, Pat accepted the promotion in 1973. It should have been the culmination of his career, but he missed the thrill of coaching. He was the athletic director, and enjoyed that responsibility. Pat still remained connected to sports as a football, basketball and baseball official. He liked making the extra pay, and loved being on the field officiating games into his seventies.

After another seven years, Pat finished his career at Pine Grove High School as the assistant principal and athletic director. His

final salary was $25,000. After 28 years of teaching, coaching and administration, Pat retired in 1979 at age 64

After retirement, Pat was one of 16 initial members inducted into the Tubby Allen - Chet Rogowicz Chapter of the Pennsylvania Sports Hall of Fame Oct 20, 1981. Among the 16 were Joe Balsis, world billiard champion, Tom

Fitzpatrick, Minersville championship basketball coach, and Jack Dolbin, (Pottsville High School) Denver Broncos receiver.

As fate would have it, "Senior Olympics" had become widespread in the 1980s and 1990s. Pat loved competition so he participated at both the county and state level. For the first time, his wife Dot and he competed together in a sport. She actually won gold medals in bowling. She was no longer a "sports widow," but now was an equal participant for the first time, with her husband. They both won gold, silver, and bronze medals. Pat displayed over 40 medals in a display case for many years.

Pat and Dot travelled extensively in their retirement, visiting their three grown children. Their adventures took them from New England to Hawaii and lots of places in between.

Pat still officiated high school football and fast pitch softball until age 75. Being a sports official was one of the most important things in Pat's life - it was a constant in all "chapters" of his life. Wearing the stripes connected him to both the players and the coaches.

When he was inducted into the Pennsylvania Sports Hall of Fame, Oct 29, 1994, Pat wrote that he considered this the "ultimate gratification, coming to me as an athlete, teacher, coach, and sports official."

The Sports Hall of Fame program read "Football – All-around sportsman, player, coach, official. 4 letterman in high school, 3 Letterman, Kutztown State College. Coached Cass Township to undefeated, unscored upon, untied season 1957. Holds State record – 15 games. Coached 2 All-State ends, 1 All-State basketball player. Coached championship teams in Football, Basketball, Baseball. PIAA official: Basketball 24 years; football 42 years. Senior Olympics: 15 medals in State; 25 on County Level"

Pat was a good Catholic. He was baptized at a very young age and attended mass at St Francis of Assisi Church, located near his home in Minersville, PA., from 1920 until 1999.

Coach Pat Droskinis handled many foes on the sports field, but he faced his toughest enemy in 1987 - cancer. Pat fought a tough battle, and thought he had the horrible disease beaten. The cancer went into remission. He had a good quality of life for another 11 years until cancer came back with a vengeance in 1998. Pat died of prostate cancer on March 23, 1999. He was 83. A few of his Cass football players served as his pall bearers. He is buried in the St. Francis Cemetery in Minersville, PA, with the inscription *"Keep the Faith."* His wife, Dot, died only a few months later and is buried beside him. Pat's grandson, Erik Droskinis, SSG, U.S. Army (Jim and Kathi Droskinis' son) tragically died at age 23, two years after Pat. His ashes are scattered there with his grandparents.

Coach Pat is gone but not forgotten. His legacy lives on thanks to of his Cass players in 1957:

UNDEFEATED UNTIED UNSCORED UPON.

Epilogue

Fun Facts and Reunions

Greatness Lasts Forever

➤ In 1958, the Cass Condors continued the '57 record of being UNSCORED UPON. The Condors went five games into the season for a combined 15 straight games, or **720 minutes** of actual game time - *12 hours* **of football without an opponent crossing their goal line!**

➤ 1957 was the first year facemasks (just a single bar) were mandated on helmets.

➤ Great players all, one small and two tall: George "Beakley" Ryan, Russ Frantz, and Harry Butsko: Beakley was only 5 ft. 5 inches, Russ and Harry were about 6 ft. 3 inches. I'd love to have a picture of the three standing together - Beakley in the middle of the "towering ends."

➤ Prior to the championship game, the Shamokin Greyhounds had already played Pottsville and beat them in a shutout 14-0. Ironically, the game was played in the mud (just as they would play against Cass in Pottsville) on Wednesday, Nov 20, 1957. But not at Pottsville. The game was played at home in Shamokin's Kemp Memorial Stadium. That is where they had hoped to play against the Northern Division champs.

➤ The Cass High Stadium lights were sold to St Clair High School. The proceeds of that sale provided 76 students a total of $57,000 over the course of 19 years. (Annual scholarship awards totaling $3,000 were given each year to four graduating students from both Minersville High and Nativity High School) Thank you Cass Township Athletic Association Scholarship Fund!

➤ When Cass played their home games on Thursday nights, they still practiced the next day after school.

➤ After each victory, WPPA, a Pottsville radio station, supplied the Cass team with a case of Coke.

➤ The Cass players told me they loved the actual games - but hated the tough practices!

➤ Pat was 42 years old when he coached Cass during that 1957 perfect season.

➤ Some of Coach Pat's favorite expressions: "We shellacked them," "Pin their ears back," and his coaching philosophy on passing versus running the ball, "When you put a football in the air (pass) *three* things can happen, and *two* of them are bad."

➤ **Coach Pat Droskinis' career**

Minersville	Feb 1950 to Jun 1954
Cass Township	Sep 1954 to Oct 1959
Schuylkill Haven	Oct 1959 to Jun 1966
Pottsville	Sep 1966 to Jun 1967
Minersville	Sep 1967 to Jun 1973
Pine Grove	Aug 1973 to Jul 1979

Cass Township Athletic Assoc. Scholarship Fund Committee

James Bergen, Harry Brennan, Monsignor Al Callaghan, Reverend Joseph Campion, Butch Condrack, Dave Gauntlett, Joe Gemmell, Gene Horan, Sylvia Jones Kanish, Katie Kirk Koperna, Paul Lohin, Ellen Ryan, James V. Ryan, Jr., Helen Socko

(**1973**) At St. Nick's Hall, Primrose L to R Frank Mitchell, Russ Frantz, Steve Yuschock, Frank Machita, Dave Gauntlett, Charlie Zurat; middle, Mike Milyo, Joe Hydock, Steve Kachmar, Gary Collins (NFL football player/guest speaker), Tony Phillips, Harry Butsko, Rich Krasnitsky; back, George Ryan, Walt Brennan, Harry Heffron, Tony Antonelli, Ed Gressik

(1987) Primrose L to R Frank Machita, Ted Wannisky, Steve Yuschock, George Ryan, Rich Krasnitsky; middle, Tony Antonelli, Steve Pecovich, Dave Gauntlett, Charlie Zurat, Harry Heffron; back, Ed Gressik, Harry Butsko, Tony Phillips, Pat Droskinis, Russ Frantz, Ron Ney

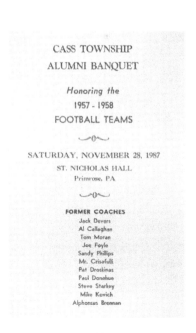

CASS TOWNSHIP
ALUMNI BANQUET

Honoring the
1957 - 1958
FOOTBALL TEAMS

SATURDAY, NOVEMBER 28, 1987
ST. NICHOLAS HALL
Primrose, PA

FORMER COACHES
Jack Devers
Al Callaghan
Tom Moran
Joe Foyle
Sandy Phillips
Mr. Crisafulli
Pat Droskinas
Paul Donahue
Steve Starkey
Mike Kovich
Alphonsus Brennan

(**1998**) 150th Cass Twp. Banquet. Representing The 1957 team at South Cass Hose Co are, L to R Charlie Zurat, Steve Yuschock, Frank Machita, Nettie Ryan (George Ryan's wife), Nelda Bower (Tom Witcofsky's goddaughter), Ray Callaghan; middle, Rose Pukas Cunningham, Barb Fatula Whelan, Joan Bower Bachman; back, Harry Butsko, Harry Heffron, Steve Pecovich, Tony Antonelli, Ed Gresik, Rich Krasnitsky, Frank Mitchell, John Pytko, Jim Heffron, Pat Droskinis

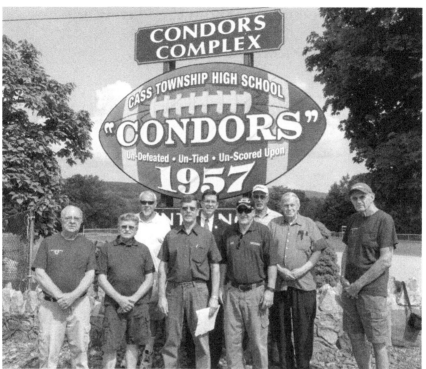

(**2015**) Primrose, sign dedication in front of old Cass school and field. L to R Frank Machita, John Hardock, John Walaitis (Cass Twp. Supv.), Jim Droskinis, Russ Frantz; back, Michael Kulpcavage (Cass Twp. Supv.),George F. Halcovage Jr.(county commissioner), Tony Phillips, Rich Krasnitsky

Appendix A (About the Players)

George "Beakley" Ryan

No one seems to know where the nickname Beakley came from. Not friends, not even his family. Beakley was only about 5 ft. 5 inches tall and all of 145 pounds. That did not prevent him from playing four years of tough football and 3 years as a catcher on the baseball team. Ryan, amazingly scored 37 points in the 1957 season, and was the second highest scorer the next year, in 1958 with eight TDs or 48 points. All the while, known to all his teammates and friends, he smoked Winston cigarettes just about every chance he could. But, that was the culture and way of life in the 1950s - hang out and smoke - there was no Surgeon General warning about cancer! No one seemed to really care, as smoking was common everywhere from restaurants to airplanes. Sadly, Ryan's smoking finally caught up to him. He died on June 27, 1998 at age 57 of lung cancer.

In high school, Beakley was a popular, dark haired, handsome guy with a 50's crew cut, and a million dollar smile. He was a mischievous kid and hailed from a small community near Minersville known as Coal Castle.

For most of his adult life, Ryan worked for Jimmy Ryan (no relation), and his son Sam, as a heavy equipment operator for Cass Contracting in Marlin, PA. Yes, the same Jimmy Ryan who was school board president at Cass.

Ryan's wonderful legacy lives on in his six children, four sons and two daughters: Joe, George, Gary, Jarrod, Rachel and Brenda.

Like their father, they all became sports stars. Beakley and his wife, Nettie (Pizzico) Ryan, hardly ever missed a game. The four boys all played varsity football at Minersville Area High School (which absorbed Cass in 1966). They even played the same positions as their father, backs and linebackers. And three of the four boys returned punts, one of the most dangerous plays in football. Years later, Jarrod told me his father (Beakley was a fearless punt return man) told them, "No fair catches! If you are gonna return punts, just catch the ball and run straight ahead."

The girls were also sports stars at Minersville High School. Rachel was a starting pitcher in fast-pitch softball, where she helped her team win two state championships. She attended Lock Haven University on a softball scholarship.

Brenda was a starting guard on the varsity basketball team, and also played softball. Her high school softball teams won one championship, but her basketball talent really paid off. She attended Bloomsburg University on a basketball scholarship.

There are 15 grandchildren. Beakley must still be smiling down on his amazing family.

Frank Machita

Frank was only a 16 year old junior in 1957, but played like a champion and he was a total team player. His teammates had no doubt about his dedication and versatility, as he was a halfback the prior season (1956), but willingly switched to blocking back or fullback at the coach's request. He still scored four touchdowns, and either kicked or ran in 14 extra points for a total of 38 points. This made him the second highest scorer on the team.

His senior year, he scored 41 points, the third highest scorer behind Gene Horan (with 49 points) and Beakley Ryan (with 48). Frank was selected to play in the Schuylkill County North-South All Star game along with teammates Joe Hydock and Harry Butsko. The great *Pottsville Republican* sports writer, Walter S. Farquhar, selected Machita to his All-County honorary football team in 1958. This was quite an honor from the longtime sports writer, Mr. Farquhar, (1888-1971) who covered the NFL Champion Pottsville Maroons in 1925. (Google "Walter S. Farquhar" for more on the legendary writer.)

Frank considered accepting football scholarship at the University of Pennsylvania, in Philadelphia, but attended Millersville State Teachers College instead. As a college freshman, he played starting linebacker on the varsity football team. Remarkably, he also played halfback on both the freshman and jayvee football teams.

After only a year of college, Frank dropped out and joined the United States Marine Corps for four years. As a Marine, he served at Paris Island, Cherry Point, Okinawa, and Quantico. Back then, all U. S. branches of service had their own sports teams and played against each other. Frank even played a bit of football as a Marine. Before returning to civilian life, he married Joan Galavage from Hecksherville in 1963.

After serving his country, Frank found his niche. He settled in for a 35-year career as an insurance adjuster, working for Ohio Casualty. He started in New York and then moved to Ohio. He and his wife Joan had two sons, Stephen and Frank. When there was an opening in Pennsylvania, Frank jumped at the opportunity to return to his roots, and built a home in Pottsville, PA in 1970. Soon after moving back home, he and Joan had one more child, this time a girl - Juliann.

In his spare time, Frank found time to volunteer in youth football. He became "coach" Machita, and helped many young boys learn sportsmanship and play football. As fate would have it, Frank coached all four of his teammate Beakley Ryan's sons.

Tragedy struck the Machita family when their son, Francis (Frank) was killed by a drunk driver in Durham, NC in 2007. He was only 39.

At the time of this edition, Frank and Joan have been married 53 years, are active and in good health. They still live in the home they built and have attended many Cass Reunions.

Charlie Zurat

If anyone typified the cooperative spirit and Cass teamwork, it was Charlie. He was always fun to be around and you could just feel his love of life. Charlie was the oldest of three kids, all boys. His brothers are Frank and John, who lived in the local area their whole lives. (Frank "Joe" also played football at Cass and as a freshman.)

Charlie was born Nov 29, 1941 and grew up in Mt. Pleasant. He was the president of his senior class. Zurat got around town driving a 1947 Chevy. He earned money in high school working for Joe Balsis meats, along with his team mates Harry Heffron, and Harry Butsko. After graduation, he was able to afford better cars, as he got a job working construction at a Philadelphia company still in existence today called *Counties*, a Danella company. He worked for them for over 20 years as an operations division manager, supervising the installation of fiber optic cable. He even became part owner at one time. Zurat retired in 2003.

Charlie lived in Marlin, PA most of his adult live. He had two children, Charlie and Alicia, and two grandchildren. Charlie is now living in Galivants Ferry, SC with his wife Stefanie. She was also a star athlete. Her sport, softball.

Dave Gauntlett

Dave was born in Chicago, Illinois on Nov 29, 1941. His parents were originally from Jonestown, PA. That is where the family lived when not traveling with his father who worked on construction. The job took his father all around the country. Whenever possible Dave, his mother and brother, John traveled with him. After living in Westerly, Rhode Island for several years, he returned to Jonestown. Dave has many fond memories of New England. He attended Cass Twp. High School and played football and basketball during his sophomore, junior, and senior years.

As you read in the chapter on "Cass Secret Weapons," Dave played a key role as the starting center on the football team both in 1957 and 1958.

Dave lives in Minersville, PA with his wife Libby and has been married over 50 years. He worked as a registered surveyor his entire career.

They have two children, Susan and Joseph. They also have five grandchildren.

Edward "Gus" Gressik

Gus was born on December 19, 1941, just six days before his uncle and team mate, Russ Frantz. Gressik always wanted to attend the U.S. Naval Academy in Annapolis, MD. As fate would have it, while he was applying and processing, he was drafted by the U.S. Navy. After his tour of duty, ended, he returned home to Schuylkill Haven Pennsylvania, and applied for a civil service position at Ft. Indiantown Gap, PA. Gus was accepted and worked there until he retired in the mid-1990s. He worked the night shift from 11PM until 7AM for 30 years.

Working nights gave Gressik plenty of time to volunteer at St. James Episcopal Church in Schuylkill Haven. He took care of their custodial and landscaping needs. Gus retained his passion for sports most of his adult life. He coached and played fast pitch softball into his 50s in local town and county leagues. Gus never married.

Tragically, Gus Gressik died suddenly of a heart attack on January 1, 2000. He was just out taking a walk, and had no symptoms. He was only 60 years old.

Harry Heffron

A 1958 Cass graduate, Harold E. Heffron was one of a few players born in the 1930s (July 6, 1939). A great team player, he blocked for others and played solid defense, yet threw more than a few touchdown passes and scored 19 points as a fullback.

The son of Mary Samilo and Joseph "Al" Heffron, Harry grew up with two brothers, John and Jim. (Jim also played on the Cass football team, as a freshman.)

During his high school years, Harry worked hard. He was one of the four Cass players (including Gressik, Zurat, and Butsko) who worked for Joe Balsis, the future world billiard champion. In the 1950s, he owned Radzievich Meats, Minersville - later called The Economy. He also helped out his father in the coal mines. Somehow, Heffron found time to play some semi-pro baseball during high school for two local teams in Hecksherville and Seltzer city to make a few extra bucks. All while playing football, basketball and baseball in high school.

After the 1957 football season, Harry was offered several football scholarships: Rutgers University, Florida State, Virginia Tech, VMI, and the University of Detroit wanted him. He accepted the offer from Detroit, and went there in the fall of 1958 with his teammate, Tony Phillips. He did not stay in Detroit because his coach did not allow him to also play varsity baseball, his favorite sport. In a weird twist of fate, his freshman football coach was Jim Leary, the son of Cass Township High School's well-liked janitor/maintenance man, Ambrose Leary.

When he returned, Harry was offered and accepted a position as a mechanic by none other than Mr. Jimmy Ryan. About a year later, Harry began his career as a heavy equipment operator for Alcon Construction, headquartered in New Jersey. Heffron operated heavy equipment his entire adult working career.

Harry married Cecelia Pizzo, whom he met at a dance at Hillcrest Hall, Minersville. They married in 1963, and they had three children, Michael, Angela, and Jayson. There are eight grandchildren.

Sadly, Harry died suddenly of an apparent brain aneurysm on September 11, 2014. He was 75 years old.

Rich Krasnitsky

After the championship game, Rich was honored to be interviewed on a local radio station, WPPA, where he spoke admiringly of his teammates. After high school, Rich worked locally in Pottsville and Reading for a few years. In 1963 Krasnitsky received his draft notice and proudly served a few years in the U.S. Army. He was stationed in Germany, where he worked as a teletype, code and radio operator.

In 1968, Rich met his future wife at a dance at the Rokosz Hotel in Minersville, PA. Her name was Anna Mary Mahoney, the daughter of longtime Cass school bus driver, Tom Mahoney, who drove a bus over 30 years between jobs at both Cass and Minersville.

Rich and Anna married in late 1968 and had two children, Joe and Maria. Maria graduated in 1989 from Nativity High School, and though Cass closed its doors in 1966, has a connection to Cass high school. She actually was one of the recipients of the Cass Township Athletic Association Scholarship Fund, set up from the sale of the Cass stadium lights. Both of their children received their Bachelor's Degrees from Albright College, Reading, PA.

After his discharge from the Army, Rich became a forklift operator with Hofmann Industries, located in Sinking Spring, PA. He was a faithful employee for almost 40 years.

Rich and Anna Mary have five grandchildren.

Joe Hydock

Joe Hydock was just a 16-year-old junior in the 1957 season, in which he was honored to have blocked the punt to win the playoff game against Shamokin. Joe did not seek glory. In fact, he converted from a back in 1956 to a lineman in 1957, as that is where the team needed him. He continued to play great football his senior year at Cass. He served in the U.S. Navy after graduation, and even did a tour of duty in Vietnam. After his honorable discharge from the Navy, Joe remained a leader and a patriot. He served as the commander of both the Marlin and the Fredericksburg American Legion posts.

He married Eileen Martin, and they had five children; three boys and two girls – Joseph (Jr), Stephen, Joe, Tracy, and Judy. Joe lived in Branchdale, PA, and commuted to New Jersey, where he worked as an electrician at the Beach Electric Corporation.

Joe died way too young on Oct 23, 1991. He bravely fought leukemia for over a year. He was only 51 years old.

Steve Yuschock

After graduation in 1958, Steve left the coal regions to serve in the U.S. Army. When he was honorably discharged, Steve settled down for life in Branchdale, PA. Steve spent his entire working career at the Extrudo/Exxon plant, Minersville, PA. Ever the sports enthusiast, Yuschock was an avid Philadelphia Eagles and Phillies fan. He spent some of his vacation time in Florida watching his Phillies during spring training.

Steve was 78 years old on his death, July 3, 2017. He never married.

Tony Phillips

Tony Phillips married his high school sweetheart, Sandy Pegarski (Class of 1959). His family name was originally "Di Filipo." That is, until his father, Anthony was told by the nuns at the catholic grade school that "Phillips" is easier. So Phillips it was.

Tony was one of five children, three boys and two girls – Emmett, Gloria, Tony, John, and Maria. They lived in Jonestown, about a mile from the Cass school. Tony's uncle was former Cass teacher and coach Sandy Phillips, who resigned in 1954 to take the head coaching job in Nutley, NJ. He remembers sitting on the bench with Coach Phillips' players in the early 1950s.

After graduation, Tony was offered a football scholarship at the University of Detroit. He accepted and played football in the fall, but came home for Thanksgiving. He never returned to college.

Tony worked in local construction for a while, until his older brother Emmett got him his first well-paying job, working on the docks in New York. He joined the Teamsters Union, and remained a loyal member for his entire 46-year career.

Tony and Sandy got married on November 23, 1963 - the day after John F. Kennedy was shot! While honeymooning in Niagara Falls, NY, Tony remembers the mood was dark and somber everywhere.

They lived in Edgewater, NJ while Tony worked for "Seatrain" as a laborer. Somehow, he learned to drive a tractor trailer by hands-on training, and he became a long haul truck driver.

In 1967, Tony and Sandy returned to Primrose and built a home. Tony drove up and down the entire East Coast for Branch Motor Freight and Roadway Express for 15 years. When a "no overnight haul" position opened up at Kane Steel, Tony drove their trucks for 31 years. Amazingly, Tony logged over three million miles in his driving career; retiring in 2006.

They have three children, Greg, Karen, and Tonya, and a total of five grandchildren.

Asked why Cass was such a great team, Tony said, "It was all about the team, not the individual. We knew one another's thoughts and worked as a unit. No stars, no me, no statistics."

Still a sportsman at heart, Tony followed his son Greg's advice, and took up golf. In his 70s, he still plays golf a few times every week.

Steve Kachmar

Steven M. Kachmar graduated from Cass with the class of 1958. He was son of the late Michael and Eva (Belas) Kachmar. They had seven children: Steven, Mary, Julia, Michael, Anna, Catherine, and Sam.

Kachmar was accepted at West Chester University. After receiving his bachelor's degree, he was not done with school. He applied to law school at Dickinson College, Carlisle, PA. After four years of hard work, Steve was awarded the Doctor of Jurisprudence (J.D.) He was an attorney and returned to Schuylkill County and passed the Pennsylvania bar exam. He set up a successful law firm on North Center Street, Pottsville, PA. Steve practiced civil and criminal law for 45 years. He also was a very successful businessman, as he owned and rented a few buildings on the main street. He never married. Steve was 71 when he died on June 12, 2011.

Theodore "Ted" Wannisky

After Ted's collarbone was broken during the fifth game of the season against Ashland, he never played football again. Always an excellent student, he focused on academics, and was the 1958 class valedictorian. Ted was rewarded with a full academic scholarship, courtesy of Alcoa Aluminum, where his father, Frank, was employed. His dad was one of a family of 11 children, and a former coal miner. Ted had a younger brother named William.

He attended Penn State University from 1958 through 1962. His major was mechanical engineering. It was such a tough curriculum that 400 students started as freshman, and only about 100 graduated. Ted was the valedictorian of that class too!

Wannisky was heavily recruited by major corporations, and accepted a position with Bell Labs (AT&T). Concurrent with his position, Ted attended the New York School of Engineering, and received his master's degree in mechanical engineering in 1964. During that busy time, working full-time and attending classes, he married Renie (Dolzani), Minersville class of 1960.

His work for Bell Labs was so critical in military systems development, that Ted was deferred from military service. He served his country in the corporate world, with a top secret clearance and helped develop the Nike-Hercules missile system. It is still in use today. His modeling and simulations work took him to Whippany, NJ.

Ted and Renie had a daughter Kristin, who graduated from Muhlenberg College, and worked as an executive banker. In a weird twist of fate, while Kristin was attending college, she met the daughter of one of the players whom Ted played against. It was Jim Trommeter, from Ashland, the same defensive end who accidentally broke Wannisky's collar bone on October 10, 1957

Ted's thirst for knowledge continued. In 1973, he received his Doctorate in Science, (a DSc is a PhD equivalent) in the thermo sciences. Ted became Dr. Wannisky.

Later in his career, Bell Labs promoted Ted to be their Director of Strategic Marketing. He worked until 1990 when he was forced into a medical retirement. Ted had suffered from a ruptured cerebral aneurysm, and was in a coma for over a week. He was lucky just to be alive.

In their retirement, Ted and his wife became avid gardeners, and loved attending Broadway plays. They have lived in the same home in Allentown, PA since 1984.

Ron "Jim" Ney

Jim Ney was the senior citizen of the team, born on June 16, 1939. He was one of seven children born to Rufus and Vern Ney. Jim's sister was the late Joan Ney, who married Jim's Cass teammate Tony Antonelli. Ney's nickname in high school was Truman (named after President Truman). After high school, Jim Ney became Airman Ney, when he joined the United States Air Force. He served for four years and was stationed in Wurtsmith Air Force Base, Oscoda, MI (near Lake Huron). While stationed there he met Fran Wolak, from Flint, MI, and they were married August 26th, 1961. They still live in Michigan in a rural area called Torch Lake, right on a golf course.

Jim was the only official Cass special teams' player. He performed kick-off duty, and also replaced the vacant guard position on 4th downs, while Gus Gressik punted. Though Jim never got credit as a starter, he played in every game.

After being honorably discharged from the USAF, Jim worked on the General Motors assembly line for the next eight years. When he had the opportunity, he took a position as a welder/metal fabricator for global company, Jervis B. Webb, in Petoskey, MI. He was a loyal employee with them for the next 28 years. Jim Ney retired in the year 2000.

Jim and Fran, married over 50 years, still travel the country and spend winters in Arizona. Jim drives a Ford diesel 350 (with a 5th wheel set-up) and pulls a 39 foot trailer. Over the years, they have logged thousands of miles. They have been as far north as Alaska, as far west as California and as far east Nova Scotia.

When not travelling, Jim plays golf a few times a week. He kiddingly told me that golf is a silly sport, "the only game where the lowest score wins," he said.

Tony "Weiner" Antonelli

Anthony Antonelli, Jr. was born on November 9, 1940. His father worked in the coal mines, and Tony helped at the mine above ground cutting timber in the early 1950s. He got the nickname "Weiner", because he spent time in the junkyard in Pottsville buying car parts. It's still there today called "Weiners." His first car at Cass was a 1948 Chevy Fleetline. Antonelli was the oldest of three children. He had a sister, Marion and a brother, Richard.

Tony was a great ball carrier for Cass, but never played varsity offense until the 1957 season. Prior to that he was purely a defensive back, but made the switch to offense when the coach asked him to try it. After that, he played both offense and defense.

A few colleges were interested in Tony and offered him a football scholarship. Virginia Tech was one. He was not interested. After high school, Tony was referred to Harrisburg by Jimmy Ryan to apply for a state civil position. He became a printer for the Pennsylvania Department of Labor and Industry, and made the drive from Minersville to Harrisburg for 35 years.

Tony married Joan Ney, the sister of one of his teammates. They had four children, all girls – the twins, Joan and Jean, Karen and Debra. Antonelli was able to retire at age 53 in 1993. He still had the same hobby of working on cars, and did a lot of that. In fact Tony is proud he "never owned a new car." He was so handy that he turned his passion into his own business, fixing lawnmowers. If it had a motor, he could fix it.

In the 1970s, when Big Diamond (the local dirt track) opened, Tony and a few friends built a race car. It was the #101, a green 1955 Chevy. They won more than a few heats. He also drove cars in demolition derbies well into his 30s.

Tony suffered a stroke in 2011. He spent over two weeks in the hospital. When he was transferred to a rehabilitation facility in Pottsville, he told the nurses, "I'll walk out of here." Being the fighter and determined fellow he is, Tony did just that! He was able to walk, and made a complete recovery.

Tony's wife, Joan passed away in May 2017 after a battle with cancer. Some of his teammates were there with him at the funeral.

Mike Milyo

Michael J. Milyo graduated from Cass High School in 1958. He only weighed about 120 pounds, but played with heart, and never missed a practice. He weighed enough to join the U.S. Marine Corps after graduation and served honorably. Mike was a marine aboard one of the support ships for the USS Essex during the Bay of Pigs invasion of Cuba in April 1961. He lived in Bonney Lake, Washington many years during his retirement.

Steve Pecovich

Steve was known as "Pancho" to his teammates. He was a very quiet guy who played football for all his four years in high school. Though he was never a starter, he was a very dependable practice player who was a tough kid. In fact, while still in high school at Cass, he joined the U.S. Marine Corps Reserve.

John Witcofsky

John was referred to as "Joe" Witcofsky in the much publicized Cass varsity photo. He is the big fellow, #29, in top right of the well-known picture. His nickname in high school was actually "Perdue". John was another tough practice player who played only one year of high school football at Cass, 1957.

Appendix B (Names and Statistics)

1957 Varsity Players
(*Returning from '56 Varsity)

	Jersey #		
Wally Brennan	10	Soph	QB
*Ted Wannisky	11	Sr	QB
*Steve Yuschock	12	Sr	G/T
George Ryan	13	Jr	B
Mike Milyo	14	Sr	HB
Rich Krasnitsky	15	Sr	G/T
*Dave Gauntlett	16	Jr	C
*Steve Kachmar (Cpt)	17	Sr	G
*Harry Heffron	18	Sr	FB
*Charlie Zurat	19	Sr	G
Frank Machita	20	Jr	FB
*Harry Butsko	21	Jr	E
*Gus Gressik (Cpt)	22	Sr	G/P
*Tony Phillips	23	Sr	T
*Joe Hydock	24	Jr	T
*Ron Ney	25	Sr	T
*Tony Antonelli	26	Sr	FB
*Steve Pecovich	27	Sr	G/T
*Russ Frantz (Cpt)	28	Sr	E
Joe Witcofsky	29	Jr	T

STARTING OFFENSE

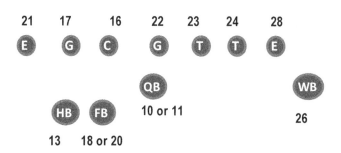

L to R, Frank Machita, Wash Brennan, Ted Wannisky, Steve Yuschock, George Ryan, Mike Milyo, Rich Krasnitsky, middle; Joe Hydock, Tony Antonelli, Steve Pecovich, Steve Kachmar, Dave Gauntlett, Charlie Zurat, Harry Heffron; back, Ed Gressik, Harry Butsko, Tony Phillips, Coach Pat Droskinis, Russ Frantz, Ron Ney, Joe Witcofsky

Cass Township Record (1957)

10-0

(PA State Eastern Conference Co-Champs with Scranton Central)

Sept. 13, 1957	Cass	27	Minersville	0
Sept. 21, 1957	Cass	32	Nescopeck	0
Sept. 26, 1957	Cass	34	W. Mahanoy Twp.	0
Oct. 3, 1957	Cass	40	Schuylkill Haven	0
Oct. 10, 1957	Cass	19	Ashland	0
Oct. 21, 1957	Cass	35	Blythe Township	0
Oct. 28, 1957	Cass	7	Mahanoy Township	0
Nov. 1, 1957	Cass	14	Lansford	0
Nov. 9, 1957	Cass	13	Saint Clair	0
Dec. 7, 1957	Cass	2	Shamokin	0
	Cass	**223**	**Opponents**	0

1957 Junior Varsity (not in order) John Hinners, Joe Zurat, George Sinko, Jack Hardock, George Gretsky, Frank Mitchell, Tom Wenner, Joe Stevens, Don Wenner, Ray Callaghan, Harry Oakhill, John Kurtak, Nick Mitchell, Dennis Onushko, Tom Kessler, Jim Heffron, Tom Jefferson, Jack Weachock, Lon Slane

Cheerleaders Rosemarie Pukas, Judy John, Barb Fatula, Sonya Talabisco, Patsy Kostick, Joan Bowers, Julianne Kowalchick, Sissy Kurilla (Mascot)

1958 Varsity
(*Returning from '57 Varsity)
Jersey

*Joe Hydock	24	Sr	LT
*Harry Butsko	28	Sr	E
*Dave Gauntlett	16	Sr	C
*George Ryan	13	Sr	LH
*Frank Machita	20	Sr	FB
*Wally Brennan	10	Jr	QB
Gene Horan	11	Sr	E
Dennis Onushko	27		LG
Joe Stevens	21		LG
Joe Zurat	25		RG
Frank Mitchell	26		RT
Ray Callaghan			HB
Jim Lucas	23	Jr	FB
George Sinko	12	Sr	HB
George Milyo			HB
John Hinners	17	Sr	G
Jack Hardock	15	Sr	G
Nick Mitchell	22	Sr	
George Gretsky	18	Sr	E
Tom Kessler	30	Jr	C
John Kurtak	27	Soph	
Tom Wenner	24	Soph	E

Cass Township Record (1958)

7-1

Sept. 12, 1958	Cass	19	Minersville	0
Sept. 18, 1958	Cass	41	Nescopeck	0
Oct. 3, 1958	Cass	32	Schuylkill Haven	0
Oct. 9, 1958	Cass	7	Ashland	0
Oct. 16, 1958	Cass	60	Blythe Township	0
Oct. 23, 1958	Cass	0	Mahanoy Twp.	6
Oct. 30, 1958	Cass	33	Lansford	0
Nov. 8, 1958	Cass	37	Saint Clair	0
	Cass	229	**Opponents**	6

Acknowledgements

I am grateful to relatives and friends who supported me during the process of researching, writing, and publishing.

➤ **Kathi Droskinis**, my wife, an avid Stephen King reader, for many hours of professional advice, exceptional editing and photography. She kept me grounded and supported the household, during my many hours away. She never complained when I "writer-hibernated," travelled, and lived on the phone.

➤ **Russ Frantz**, team co-captain (Cass class of 1958), who organized team meetings, contacted teammates about details, and did anything else needed to get the book done. He organized Cass football team reunions, spent hours on the phone with me, and even allowed me to stay with him a few times on my multiple trips to Pennsylvania.

➤ **Frank Machita**, team fullback (Cass class of 1959), for sharing material from the scrapbook that his sister and mom kept all those years. He shared his photos, and offered guidance, feedback and advice as I worked through all the games. What a memory Frank has!

➤ **Charlie Zurat**, team linebacker (Cass class of 1958), for his kind assistance in many technical aspects about "defense," specific games, and for his encouragement and friendship.

➤ *The Republican-Herald* **(formerly called** *The Pottsville Republican*), the daily newspaper that covered Cass sports early and often. The sports staff was always kind to Cass and educated new generations of readers on the amazing accomplishments of Cass teams. They covered not just the 1957 and '58 football teams, but also the contributions of Cass over many decades.

➤ **Minersville American Legion Post 544**, for their longtime support and recognition of Cass Township happenings. (building torn down in 2017)

➢ **South Cass Citizens' Fire Company,** for their ongoing support of Cass Township and the display case featuring Cass High School athletic memorabilia.

➢ **Diane (Stevenosky) Jenkins**, (Cass class of 1959) my "research assistant" (unpaid), and collector of "all things Cass." Without Diane's Cass yearbook collection, booklets, pictures, and her legwork gathering information, this book would have been impossible. Her moral support kept my spirits up.

➢ **Sylvania (Jones) Kanish**, (Cass class of 1958) who tirelessly organizes countless Cass reunions year after year for hundreds of Cass grads, always honoring the football team.

➢ **Dawn (Droskinis) Rodrigues**, Coach Pat's daughter, and my big sister. Dawn has written several books, edited many, and performed much-needed final edits on this one.

➢ **Jon (Droskinis) Peterson**, Coach Pat's other son, and my younger brother. He added much to Chapter 1, the Introduction, and Chapter 23, on our dad. He advised me, edited in his unique way, and always encouraged me to "keep the faith" in writing this book. Jon provided many of the "Coach Pat" photos.

Also, thanks to my little 14-year old best buddy, *Rand*, who kept me company in my windowless basement office - many long hours!

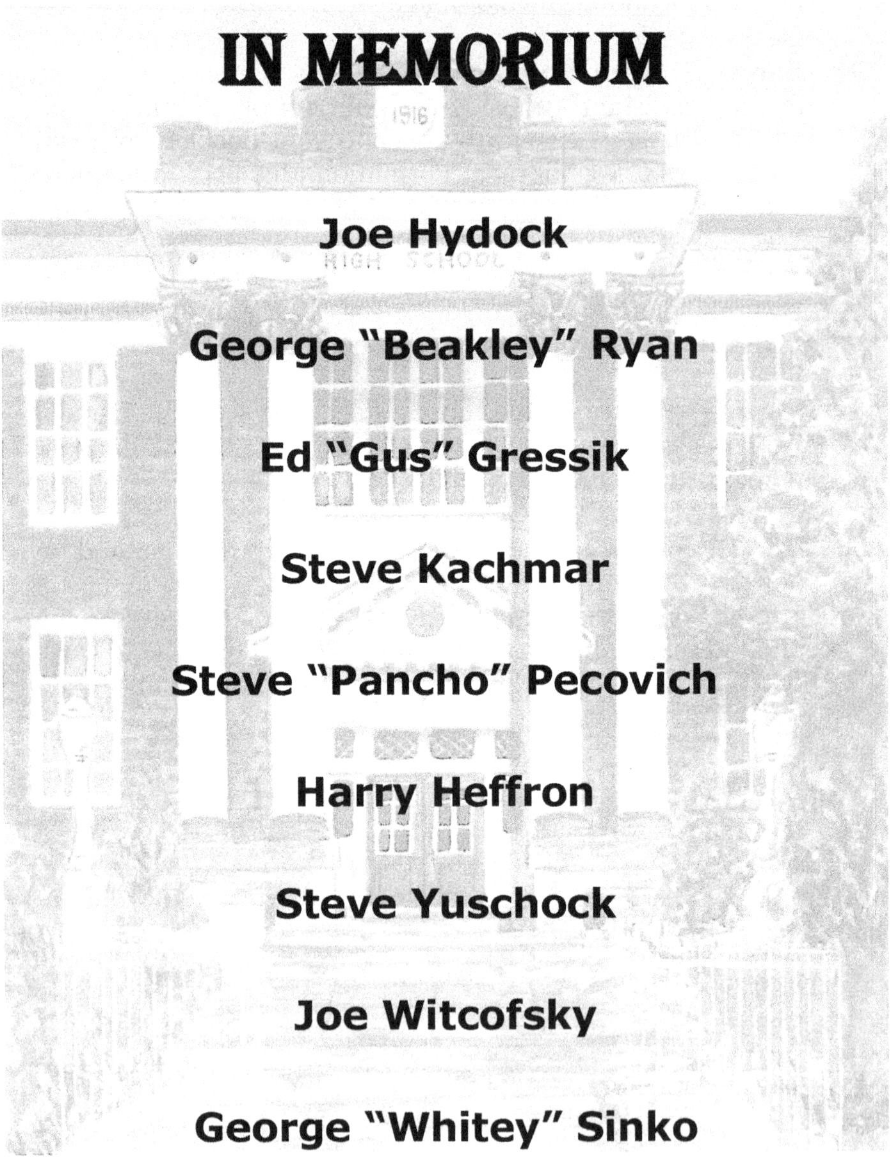

IN MEMORIUM

Joe Hydock

George "Beakley" Ryan

Ed "Gus" Gressik

Steve Kachmar

Steve "Pancho" Pecovich

Harry Heffron

Steve Yuschock

Joe Witcofsky

George "Whitey" Sinko

CASS TOWNSHIP HIGH SCHOOL

Made in United States
Orlando, FL
13 July 2022

19734400R00098